T0328443

Cambridge Elements

Elements in American Politics
edited by
Frances E. Lee
Princeton University

THE STUDY OF US STATE POLICY DIFFUSION

What Hath Walker Wrought?

Christopher Z. Mooney
University of Illinois, Chicago

CAMBRIDGE
UNIVERSITY PRESS

CAMBRIDGE
UNIVERSITY PRESS

University Printing House, Cambridge CB2 8BS, United Kingdom

One Liberty Plaza, 20th Floor, New York, NY 10006, USA

477 Williamstown Road, Port Melbourne, VIC 3207, Australia

314–321, 3rd Floor, Plot 3, Splendor Forum, Jasola District Centre,
New Delhi – 110025, India

79 Anson Road, #06–04/06, Singapore 079906

Cambridge University Press is part of the University of Cambridge.

It furthers the University's mission by disseminating knowledge in the pursuit of education, learning, and research at the highest international levels of excellence.

www.cambridge.org
Information on this title: www.cambridge.org/9781108958325
DOI: 10.1017/9781108956017

First published 2020

A catalogue record for this publication is available from the British Library.

ISBN 978-1-108-95832-5 Paperback
ISSN 2515-1606 (online)
ISSN 2515-1592 (print)

Cambridge University Press has no responsibility for the persistence or accuracy of URLs for external or third-party internet websites referred to in this publication and does not guarantee that any content on such websites is, or will remain, accurate or appropriate.

The Study of US State Policy Diffusion

What Hath Walker Wrought?

Elements in American Politics

DOI: 10.1017/9781108956017
First published online: December 2020

Christopher Z. Mooney
University of Illinois, Chicago
Author for correspondence: Christopher Z. Mooney, cmoon1@uic.edu

Abstract: In 1969, political scientist Jack Walker published "The Diffusion of Innovations among the American States" in the *American Political Science Review.* "Walker 1969" has since become a cornerstone of political science, packed with ideas, conjectures, and suggestions that spawned multiple lines of research in multiple fields. In good Kuhnian fashion, Walker 1969 is important less for the answers it provides than for the questions it raises, inspiring generations of political scientists to use the political, institutional, and policy differences among the states to understand policymaking better. Walker 1969 is the rock on which the modern subfield of state politics scholarship was built, in addition to inspiring copious research into federalism, comparative politics, and international relations. This Element documents the deep and extensive impact of Walker 1969 on the study of policymaking in the US states. In the process, it organizes and analyzes that literature, demonstrating its progress and promise.

Keywords: policy diffusion, state politics, federalism, innovation diffusion, public policy, Jack Walker

ISBNs: 9781108958325 (PB), 9781108956017 (OC)
ISSNs: 2515-1606 (online), 2515-1592 (print)

Contents

1 Introduction

In September 1969, the *American Political Science Review* published "The Diffusion of Innovations among the American States," by University of Michigan political scientist Jack Walker. This paper had multiple, overlapping, and diverse questions, featured uncertain and less-than-precise empirical results, was written in the pre-word-processing era of less-than-tight editing, and imported a theory of behavior that, while new to political science, had been used widely in various social sciences for almost a century. Even the general question Walker posed was an old one in the discipline: Why does a government enact the policies that it does?

Despite this unpromising start, "Walker 1969" became one of the most important papers ever published in political science, one whose impact remains vital and expansive even today, more than fifty years after publication. Walker simultaneously co-opted that decades-old, multidisciplinary, theoretical tradition and shifted the attention slightly to ask the question: How is policymaking in one government affected by the actions of other governments? That is, what are the *interdependencies* among governments' policies, especially when there is no formal, hierarchical power relationship involved? Walker wondered whether the adoption of a policy by one state could affect the odds of another state adopting that policy. Or, as it has been characterized by generations of scholars, how does policy "diffuse" across the US states?

Walker 1969 identified a particularly interesting and problematic set of research questions. In a federal system, the vertical and horizontal relationships among governments are often a matter of contentious policy debate, among both policymakers and political scientists. The USA is one of the most mature and largest federal systems in the world, making it an excellent venue for research into these issues. Certainly, the Founders debated intensely the relationship between the states and the national government (Bailyn and Allison 2018). On the other hand, the horizontal relationships among the states remain informal,[1] with the US Constitution largely silent on the issue. The states are established as peers, equal to one another (at least in terms of US Senate representation and a few other important duties), and with a few restrictions to prevent interstate discrimination.

Despite this constitutional vagueness, the states sit cheek-to-jowl with one another, with overlapping media markets, free flow of people and goods across borders, a lingua franca, and a common culture and overarching political system, so a state's policies might be influenced by the actions of its peers,

---

[1] Interstate compacts are a formal way for states to structure their relationships (Nicholson-Crotty et al. 2014), but these are ad hoc and limited relative to the vast range of US domestic policy.

however informally. Beyond the USA, scholarly and practical interest in inter-governmental relations has soared internationally in recent decades within federalist countries like Canada and India, but also with the collapse of one major federal system (the USSR) and the rise of another (the European Union) (Stepan 1999; Trechsel 2006).

By raising this question of policy interdependence, Walker 1969 helped define the subfield of state politics and policy in political science. Today, this subfield flourishes, with its own journal (*State Politics and Policy Quarterly*), a twenty-year series of annual conferences, and one of the most active organized sections of the American Political Science Association (APSA). Certainly, political scientists studied the US states before Walker 1969. Some examined how the states and regions differed from one another in their politics and policy (e.g., Fenton 1966; Key 1949; Lockard 1959), while others used the states as convenient, numerous, and comparable cases to test general hypotheses about policymaking (e.g., Dawson and Robinson 1963; Fabricant 1952; Hofferbert 1966; Sharkansky 1968). But by highlighting policy interdependence, Walker 1969 identified a research subject that, if not exclusive to the states, certainly made them a uniquely appropriate venue for research. Focus on policy inter-dependence among the states gave the field definition and drive. Today, the field of state politics and policy remains largely, if not solely, distinguished from other fields by this focus. Many scholars continue to use these fifty comparable cases to test hypotheses generated elsewhere (e.g., Anzia and Jackman 2013; Barwick and Dawkins 2020; Burstein 2020; Crabtree and Nelson 2019; Filindra 2013; Soss et al. 2001). But the central distinguishing feature of the state politics and policy literature is the ever-expanding interest in the policy relationships among the states. Walker 1969 is the foundation of that literature.

What differentiates the study of state policy diffusion from that of federal-ism? This is an old question in political science. For instance, in 1990, when the APSA's Council considered the application for a State Politics and Policy organized section, venerable scholar Nelson Polsby raised the objection that since there was already a Federalism section, the new one would be redundant (Virginia Gray personal communication). Polsby lost that argument. Of course, scholarship on politics and policy in the American states includes more than just policy diffusion research. But for those studying governmental interdependen-cies, the distinction between federalism and diffusion is not categorical but rather one of emphasis. For instance, state policy diffusion studies tend to focus on horizontal relations among governments, while federalism studies tend to emphasize national–regional hierarchical relationships (e.g, Grodzins 1966; Karch and Rose 2019; Michener 2018). The distinction is largely about intel-lectual tradition, and this essay maps out the tradition associated with policy diffusion. There is much overlap and complementarity between the federalism and diffusion literatures.

Walker 1969 was first cited by another study less than one year after its publication (Fry and Winters 1970), but it was also quickly and directly challenged (Eyestone 1977; Gray 1973a; Rose 1973). These controversies, along with several early follow-up studies (e.g., Foster 1978; Grupp and Richards 1975; Savage 1978), led to a multi-decade burst of research productivity and creativity rarely seen in political science. Today, Walker 1969 is the eighth most-cited article ever published in the *APSR*.[2] It stands at the core of the state politics and policy subfield, as well as generating major lines of research in comparative politics and international relations (Simmons and Elkins 2004; Tien 2015; Weyland 2009). Walker 1969 is the archetypal seminal article and one of the most significant pieces of political science ever published.

This essay is not a comprehensive survey of the scholarship on state policy diffusion that flowed from Walker 1969. Rather, it examines illustrative studies in the evolution of this literature, with emphasis on recent works, so as to organize and explain this literature. Such organization and self-reflection are greatly needed at this moment in the field's history. As described herein, the study of state policy diffusion has developed and expanded considerably in the twenty-first century. A series of key studies in the 2000s (e.g., Boehmke 2009a; Boehmke and Witmer 2004; Braun and Gilardi 2006; Gilardi 2010; Grossback, Nicholson-Crotty, and Peterson 2004; Volden 2006; Volden, Ting, and Carpenter 2008) clearly showed the potential for the diffusion phenomenon to shed light on many aspects of policymaking, while also developing the theoretical and methodological approaches needed to accomplish this. In response, the 2010s saw a plethora of young scholars pushing the boundaries of our knowledge on many fronts using state policy diffusion (e.g., Boushey 2016; Desmarais, Harden, and Boehmke 2015; Hannah and Mallinson 2018; Jansa, Hansen, and Gray 2019; Kreitzer 2015; Kroeger 2016; Pacheco 2012; Parinandi 2020). Thus, the need for this essay stems from the enormous success of Walker 1969 in inspiring political scientists even today. I place these studies into context, chart out various lines of thought, and demonstrate connections between different aspects of the policymaking process that state policy diffusion scholarship highlights. Of course, this essay will be out of date upon the publication of the next issue of *American Journal of Political Science* or *State Politics and Policy Quarterly*. But consolidating and taking stock of this

---

[2] This ranking is based on Google Scholar citations as of January 1, 2020. Cambridge Core Listing shows Walker 1969 as the twelfth most-cited *APSR* article, based on the Social Science Citation Index.

literature now should give strong guidance for scholars working these fields for some years to come.[3]

How could a paper using an unproven and ultimately problematic research approach, with less-than-precise empirical results, that was not especially central to its author's core research agenda, and that he did not follow up on extensively, become so central to the discipline? The general answer comes from Kuhn (1970): good questions often stimulate more progressive research than do clear answers. And Walker 1969 asked some darned productive questions.

1.1 The Intellectual Roots of Walker 1969

Walker focused on "one of the most fundamental policy decisions of all: whether to initiate a program" (1969: 880). This is among the most basic topics for political science. For his study, Walker drew on two major lines of scholarship, one within political science and one multidisciplinary.

First, Walker wrote in direct response to a once-prominent political science literature, studies of whether economic or political factors matter most in determining policy (see Fenton and Chamberlayne 1969 and Dye 1979 for reviews). This literature boasts some of the earliest uses of multivariate analysis in the discipline. Economist Solomon Fabricant (1952) initiated the discussion by using state government expenditure data as policy output measures. He concluded that, controlling for socioeconomic factors, politics have no independent effect on policy. Foundational qualitative studies of the states had argued otherwise (e.g., Fenton 1966; Key 1949; Lockard 1959), so political scientists were puzzled – and challenged. As a result, scholars spent the 1960s using quantitative methods searching (largely in vain) for any independent impact of politics or political institutions on state government spending (Dawson and Robinson 1963; Dye 1966, 1984; Hofferbert 1966; Sharkansky 1968). These scholars used the states as their unit of analysis due to their unique comparability as fifty distinct governments (Mooney 2001b). Walker called this "a notable revival of interest in the politics of the American states" (1969: 880).

Walker approached this literature skeptically. Expenditure measures of policy output have an intuitive appeal, and comparable data are readily available. But just as this "SES vs political institutions" literature flourished, an influential literature on decision-making developed that challenged the validity of these

---

[3] For discussions of the copious work on policy diffusion in comparative politics and international relations, see Graham, Shipan, and Volden 2013; Simmons and Elkins 2004; Tien 2015; Weyland 2009. Likewise, there are parallel literatures on the internal determinants of policy (Burstein 2020) and international policy transfer (Dolowitz and Marsh 1996; Minkman, van Buuren, and Bekkers 2018) to which Walker 1969 contributed significantly.

measures of policy. This literature argued that time, budget, and information constraints lead to budgetary incrementalism, breaking the direct link between budget figures and policy effort (e.g., Lindblom 1959; Simon 1969; Wildavsky 1964). Political scientists needed a better indicator of policy output to study why policymakers make the decisions they do. This was Walker's challenge.

To do so, Walker co-opted a well-developed research tradition from other social sciences – the study of the diffusion of new ideas, or "innovations." Developed by anthropologists and sociologists in the late nineteenth and early twentieth centuries (e.g., Davis 1930; McVoy 1940; Tarde 1903; see Katz, Levin, and Hamilton 1963 for a review), innovation diffusion theory is based on the same insight as incrementalism theory: when decision makers are overwhelmed with options and information, they adopt cognitive shortcuts to make satisfactory choices (Simon 1969). Incrementalism is one such shortcut, but others may exist, such as taking cues from peers. As decision makers adopt a policy they see elsewhere, and as others further adopt it based on that adoption, and so on, the innovation "diffuses" among the people or institutions involved. Diffusion was typically associated with geography, with decision makers looking for lessons near to home. From water sterilization in Peruvian villages to hybrid seed usage on Iowa farms, a vast literature has explored the human tendency to facilitate decision-making by seeing what the neighbors are doing (see Rogers 2003 for an extensive review).

In addition to this theoretical choice, Walker made a methodological choice that has reverberated through the discipline for half a century. Instead of readily available state expenditure data, Walker studied the initial adoption of qualitatively new policy in a state. In other words, he studied innovation, as did the multidisciplinary diffusion literature (Rogers 2003). To do this, Walker reconceptualized his variables and determined the dates that the various states adopted a given policy. In the process, *Walker's unit of analysis became the innovation diffusion itself*. That is, he tried to explain the sequence of adoptions of a new policy among the states. This reconceptualization of policy output purged the accumulation of old decisions and compromises that incremental budgeting represents, allowing for a more precise assessment of policymaking influences. Innovation may also heighten policymakers' attention because of the visibility and risk of a new policy (Mohr 1969). Walker examined eighty-eight such policy diffusions, seeking patterns to help understand why states adopted innovations when they did.

While it facilitated copious scholarship, Walker's choice to study policy adoption came at a cost that the field still pays today, including a bias toward studying policies that diffuse widely (Karch et al. 2016; Volden 2016). Focusing on adoptions can hide differences among bills, large or small. Concentrating on the binary adoption distinction has led the field to understudy policy content, in general. The adoption focus also led scholars to emphasize legislatively passed bills, whereas judges, bureaucrats, and voters set much state policy. Other stages of the policymaking process are given shorter shrift by this focus, such as agenda setting and policy development. Throughout this essay, I highlight lines of inquiry that attempt to address these issues, but many opportunities still exist.

Walker argued that "state officials make most of their decisions by analogy" (1969: 889), observing other governments for potential solutions to their common problems. The most obvious analogs are their sister states, with parallel roles in American government, broadly similar institutions and political cultures, and being linked horizontally in a federal system. In particular, Walker reasoned that state policymakers use their *geographical neighbors* as models, perhaps along with certain national leaders. Their neighbors are those states with which they are most familiar, have regular communications and interactions, and often share many characteristics. From this, Walker (1973: 1187) envisioned policy diffusion as "a succession of spreading ink-blots on a map." This image had strong verisimilitude for students of state government, and it sparked the scholarly imagination of the field. Walker formulated the idea as a junior faculty member supervising legislative interns in Lansing (Baumgartner 2006). He noticed that perhaps the most common state legislative information request is, "What are other states doing on this issue, especially our neighboring states?"

Just as their quantity, comparability, and data availability made the states an excellent venue for expenditure studies, they are also an excellent place to study the general question of policy diffusion. The states are structurally parallel, with many more cultural, economic, and political similarities than either national or local governments. Thus, the states provide enough variation on key variables to yield empirical leverage on policy adoption questions, but without so much extraneous noise that it drowns out the diffusion signal (Mooney 2001b). The federal relationship among the various governments in the USA also added interest to the analysis. In the states, Walker found an excellent venue to study the question of how governments influence one another's decision-making.

Walker's simple insight divined from qualitative observation, along with supporting data from his eighty-eight diffusions, have since launched thousands of studies. I say "insight" because it was certainly less Walker's data than his ideas that caught scholars' attention. While his original eighty-eight policy diffusions have been subsumed into the massive common dataset of diffusions used by scholars today (Boehmke et al. 2020), Walker's methods and specific conclusions are no longer directly relevant to the field. Rather, it has been the theoretical idea of diffusion and the various questions and implications he derived from it that sparked such enormous scholarly interest. While geographic policy diffusion may seem plausible, its existence raises many significant theoretical questions: How do policies diffuse among the states? Do states learn from one another, are they in competition, or are they merely copying each other? To what extent can we talk about policies "moving" from one state to the next? Are geographic adoption patterns spurious, due to similar states adopting similar policies? What else influences policy adoption, and how can we control for that? Why do some policies diffuse quickly while others do so more slowly? Why are some states innovators and others laggards? How does federalism affect diffusion? Do states customize the policies they adopt? More generally, given that individual behavior is the motive force behind diffusion theory, are we committing an ecological fallacy by inferring it from group behavior, like policymaking (Robinson 1950; Rose 1973)? Walker 1969 generated these and other research questions, many of which scholars extrapolated. As Kuhn 1970 teaches, the most potent scientific studies are often those that raise good questions and provide the opportunity for future research, rather than those that give a definitive answer to a single research question. This is the genius of Walker 1969.

1.2 The Place of Walker 1969 in Political Science

How can we gauge the significance of a piece of scholarship to its field? One oft-used approach is through its citations in subsequently published works, a standard, if imperfect, indicator of impact on the scientific conversation (Atchison 2017; Graham, Shipan, and Volden 2013; Kim and Grofman 2019).[4]

As of January 1, 2020, Walker 1969 had been cited in published scholarship 3,104 times; even fifty years after publication, the paper generates a steady stream of more than 150 citations annually. To place these numbers in context, consider several other foundational works in state politics. The top section of Table 1 shows that Walker 1969 is one of two exceptionally well-cited state politics classics, along with Elazar's *American Federalism*. Like *Statehouse Democracy*, *American Federalism* garners many citations from its important work developing a widely used measure (i.e., Elazar's measures of state political subcultures). Two other heavily cited works (Berry and Berry 1990 and Gray 1973a) are direct extensions of and/or controversies with Walker 1969 itself. Finally, *Southern Politics*, *Statehouse Democracy,* and *American Federalism* are book-length works with a wide variety of insights and questions, spawning significant follow-up research.

---

[4] For citation data, I use Google Scholar for convenience and comparability.

Table 1 Citations of example seminal political science scholarship

	Citations
Walker 1969	3104
State Politics Scholarship	
Berry and Berry, "State Lottery Adoptions"	1913
Elazar, *American Federalism*	3196
Erikson, Wright, and McIver, *Statehouse Democracy*	1931
Gray, "Innovation in the States"	1660
Key, *Southern Politics*	1072
Other Seminal American Politics Scholarship	
Dahl, *Who Governs?*	9531
Baumgartner and Jones, *Agenda and Instability in American Politics*	8484
Lowi, *The End of Liberalism*	4284
Mayhew, *Congress: The Electoral Connection*	8330

Source: Google Scholar, January 1, 2020

Walker 1969 is unique in this group in terms of (a) being article length and (b) providing no widely used new measures.[5] Furthermore, while methodology has been debated in the state policy diffusion literature over the years (see Section 3.5), references to Walker 1969 in the past twenty-five years generally are substantive. Walker's questions and ideas, rather than his method, data, or findings, are what continue to inspire scholars.

The bottom half of Table 1 displays citation levels for four other seminal American political science studies from various eras, some of the most significant in the discipline. These books are all clearly better cited than Walker 1969, but given their greater subject matter breadth, the order of magnitude is not far off. These four books did much of what Walker 1969 did, raising a variety of new questions, bringing in theoretical perspectives from outside political science, and provoking controversy upon publication. Like Walker 1969, these works became seminal because of their ideas, not their specific results. They posed provocative questions, shined light on unexplored phenomena, and inspired young scholars to follow them. Spurring young scholars to take a new path is the hallmark of foundational scholarship (Kuhn 1970).

The pattern of Walker 1969's citations over time further demonstrates its scholarly significance. In the 1970s and 1980s, scholars began probing some of Walker's ideas (e.g., Clark 1985; Foster 1978; Gray 1973a; Savage 1978, 1985),

---

[5] Walker 1969's measure of state "innovativeness" spawned a thin line of subsequent research (see Section 3.2.1). But that measure is not the reason for the vast majority of its citations.

but two papers published within one year of each other in the early 1990s directly expanded the impact of Walker 1969. Berry and Berry 1990 introduced theory and method to model internal and external policy adoption simultaneously (event history analysis – EHA), and Rose 1991 introduced the idea of diffusion (or "lesson drawing") to the comparative policy field. These papers are themselves seminal, each being cited more than 1,500 times and spawning a great leap of interest in this subject. From 1969 to 1990, Walker 1969 was cited 446 times – a substantial number for that period. But over the subsequent twenty-two years, Walker 1969 earned 1,530 citations. Walker 1969 was cited twice as often in the 2000s as in the 1990s, and the 2010s saw another near doubling, demonstrating the exponential citation growth typical of highly influential scholarship (Sigelman 2006). This citation pattern reflects the resurgence of interest in policy diffusion scholarship generated by Berry and Berry 1990 and Rose 1991, along with that of a third generation of seminal diffusion papers published in the 2000s (e.g., Boehmke and Witmer 2004; Grossback, Nicholson-Crotty, and Peterson 2004; Karch 2007; Simmons and Elkins 2004; Shipan and Volden 2006; Volden 2006; Volden, Ting, and Carpenter 2008; Weyland 2005).

In short, Walker 1969 is among the most important scholarly works in the political science canon. This is especially remarkable because it was not a lengthy book, nor was it the culmination of a long research agenda, nor did Walker follow it up much in related works. Each of the other classic works in Table 1 has one or more of these characteristics. As such, Walker 1969 is especially remarkable for the power of its ideas – and for the wide range of interesting questions it posed.

1.3 What Is Policy Diffusion?

Walker's shift of focus from government spending to policy innovation adoption fundamentally shifted the state politics research agenda by raising new and interesting questions, especially about *external influences* on state policy. Expenditure studies focused largely on policy determinants internal to a state – i.e., its socioeconomic and political characteristics – but thinking about innovation begs the question of where the state got a new idea in the first place (Parinandi 2020). While policy ideas may come from within a state (Shipan and Volden 2006), Walker suggested that other states may be good sources of policy ideas, with theoretical support from the multidisciplinary diffusion literature (Rogers 2003). In particular, drawing on the literature on decision-making under uncertainty (e.g., Lindblom 1959; Simon 1969) and observing that policy innovations spread like "ink-blots" across the US map (Walker 1973: 1187), Walker suggested that states take policy cues from their neighboring states and national leaders. The state policy diffusion literature has since focused its principal attention on external policy influences.

This line of thought resonated with scholars because interdependence is one of the "defining features of politics," both in terms of strategic behavior and information flow in decision-making (Gilardi 2010: 650). Politics are relational, and recent state policy adoption scholarship has highlighted this using network analysis (Desmarais, Harden, and Boehmke 2015; Garrett and Jansa 2015). The empirical regularity of diffusion "ink-blots" also suggests interdependence – states may gather policy information and guidance from their neighbors. As Berry and Berry (1990: 400) wrote, "policy adoptions by nearby states provide a critical (information) resource for overcoming an obstacle (uncertainty) to innovation." Rose (1991: 13) agrees: "the basic decision rule is . . . start searching near at hand." Such thinking is rooted in Simon's 1969 seminal concept of "satisficing," where decision makers with limited time and information settle for "good enough" choices rather than optimal ones. Subsequent research has developed this line of thought very broadly (Kahneman 2011), suggesting that familiarity and availability (neighboring states) and attention and salience (national leader states) can lead one state's policy to influence another's (Boushey 2010; Karch 2007a; Mooney 2001a; Weyland 2009).

Walker's intuitive ink-blots – coupled with this strong theoretical argument – led generations of scholars to account for interstate proximity in state policy innovation models with indicators of neighboring or co-regional states that had previously adopted the policy. Yet after decades of research and hundreds of estimated models, scholars still debate the appropriate proximity indicator and even whether proximity matters at all. While some argue that "there is a general consensus that states may look to neighboring states to inform their own policy decisions" (Fay and Wenger 2016: 351), others have found either no such consensus (Allen, Pettus, and Haider-Markel 2004; Mooney 2001a) or that the effect fades over time (Leiser 2017; Lutz 1987; Shipan and Volden 2012; Welch and Thompson 1980). Furthermore, while "proximity" is typically assumed to influence innovation positively in this literature (i.e., a neighbor's adoption increases your odds of adoption), it may sometimes have a negative influence (Bromley-Trujillo and Karch 2020; Mooney 2001a; Soule and Earl 2001; Strang and Tuma 1993). The literature is further complicated by the variety of "proximity" indicators used in these studies, such as the number of (or percentage of, or any) neighboring states (or co-regional states) having the policy. Measurement issues like arbitrary regional definitions, varying border lengths, and uneven population distributions have challenged policy diffusion scholars (Berry and Baybeck 2005;

Caldeira 1985; Sharkansky 1968). Beyond these issues, any proximity relationship could be spurious if neighboring states' similar characteristics cause them to adopt similar policies independently, the so-called "Galton's problem" of homophily (Braun and Gilardi 2006; see also Lutz 1987; Rose 1973; and Volden, Ting, and Carpenter 2008).

The fundamental theoretical question that most state policy diffusion scholars have been grappling with in the past two decades is, even if empirical regularities like the ink-blots do exist, *what interstate processes cause them?* Much early theorizing about diffusion causal mechanisms was vague, cursory, and conflicting. As Karch (2007b: 56) noted, "one of the starkest shortcomings of [then-] existing state policy diffusion research is that it focuses almost exclusively on geographical proximity" without trying to understand what causes this pattern. Likewise, Strang and Soule (1998: 275) write in the sociology literature on diffusion that "no distinctive logic can be proposed – rather spatial proximity facilitates all kinds of interactions and influence." In other words, if policy interdependency exists among the states, what is the causal mechanism behind it? The current generation of state policy scholars has attacked this question with gusto. In the next section, I discuss the research and theory into the potential causal mechanisms of *learning, competition, emulation,* and *coercion* (Gilardi and Wasserfallen 2019; Graham, Shipan, and Volden 2013; LaCombe and Boehmke 2020).

2 Mechanisms of Policy Diffusion

What causes state policy diffusion? What processes are at work behind these spreading ink-blots? While copious papers have hypothesized – and some have found evidence for – geography-based patterns of adoption, the theoretical arguments behind them were often conflicting and vague in the early literature following Walker 1969. Even the indicators of innovator proximity used in these studies were "unstable, unspecified, and occasionally overlapping" (Maggetti and Gilardi 2016: 102). As Gilardi (2016: 9) puts it, "research in many areas has established that diffusion is a real phenomenon. [But] moving beyond this basic finding has proven difficult."

LaCombe and Boehmke (2020: 22) argue that "the ability to identify the presence of a distinct mechanism of diffusion ... requires careful thinking about how theoretical concepts map into measures." Early state policy diffusion scholars often glossed over the finer points of the hypothesized causal mechanism (e.g., Foster 1978; Lutz 1986, 1987). Walker 1969 mentions learning, emulation, and competition as ways neighboring states might influence each other, but he does not develop or test these ideas. While scholars recognized early that multiple mechanisms could cause state policy diffusion (Eyestone

1977), the first sustained efforts to sort them out empirically did not come until the 2000s (Berry and Baybeck 2005; Boehmke and Witmer 2004; Shipan and Volden 2008; Volden 2006). Recently, studies have even found multiple causal mechanisms at work in a given policy diffusion (Bouche and Volden 2011; Shipan and Volden 2008). As Mallinson (2020a: 28) writes, "determining the mechanism of adoption for a given policy is not simple," neither theoretically nor empirically.

Causal thinking is critical for explanation. For example, some state policy scholars have used an epidemiological analogy for diffusion, where innovations act as a "disease" that spreads from one entity to another in close proximity (Boushey 2010; Karch 2007a; Rogers 2003; Soule and Earl 2001). While this provides an intuitive empirical analogy to spreading policy ink-blots, its appeal faded as scholars thought more critically about causation.[6] Most obviously, state policy is made by intentional human actors, not viruses. While Pacheco (2011) explores "social contagion" in diffusion through elected officials' responses to public opinion, scholars have used the disease analogy largely for convenience rather than for any detailed substantive lessons. Since Walker 1969, scholars have considered a wide variety of potential causal explanations for state policy diffusion, each with its own explanatory logic.[7] In the following, I review the literature on the four mechanisms most widely discussed in the state policy diffusion literature: learning, competition, emulation, and coercion (Drolc, Ganrud, and Williams 2020; Gilardi and Wasserfallen 2019; Graham, Shipan, and Volden 2013; LaCombe and Boehmke 2020).

2.1 Learning

A policy may diffuse as a state's policymakers learn from other states' experiences with it, applying lessons about its impacts elsewhere to their own state (Bouche and Volden 2011; Minkman, van Buuren, and Bekkers 2018; Rose 1991; Stone 1999). This idea has great normative appeal, often touted as a benefit of federalism (Volden, Ting, and Carpenter 2008). State policy diffusion scholars regularly invoke the notion of states as "laboratories of democracy," following Associate Justice of the US Supreme Court Louis Brandeis (*New State Ice House Co.* v. *Liebmann* 932): "It is one of the happy incidents of the federal system that a single courageous state may, if its citizens choose, serve as a laboratory; and try novel social and economic experiments without risk to the rest of the country." In other words, state-level trial and error may

---

[6] See Boushey 2012 for a thoughtful study that uses the disease analogy fruitfully.

[7] Graham, Shipan, and Volden (2012: 690) found 104 different words used for diffusion-related processes in the literature.

lead to more rational and effective policy as information about its impacts spreads around the country (Bouche and Volden 2011; Macinko and Silver 2015; Shipan and Volden 2008, 2012). Of course, this naïve rationalism requires the assumption that "if evaluators agree that the policy achieves its stated goals, other states will enact an identical program once they are made aware of the achievement" (Karch 2007a: 5). While it is unlikely that state policymakers always agree on policy goals, learning may occur even among a subset of them with shared goals.

Learning's normative appeal helped lead early state policy diffusion scholars – including Walker – often to conflate all diffusion with learning (e.g., Balla 2001; Eyestone 1977; Foster 1978; Grupp and Richards 1975). But learning is very different from competition and the other hypothesized diffusion mechanisms, in both its mechanics and its normative implications. I analyze the treatment of learning in this literature using five questions: (1) what is learning?, (2) who learns?, (3) what is learned?, (4) whom is it learned from?, and (5) how can we observe learning?

2.1.1 What Is Learning?

After decades of confounding learning with other mechanisms, scholars began in earnest to differentiate and understand learning in state policy diffusion following Volden's highly influential 2006 paper. And even today, while the language of the diffusion literature often implies macro-level learning (i.e., the states "learn"), diffusion scholars have tended to theorize about micro-level learning – how do *people* learn? Micro-level learning has been considered from at least two perspectives: Bayesian analysis and bounded rationality.

Bayesian analysis provides a general theory of rational learning: new information is weighted by one's prior beliefs, leading to improved, updated beliefs (Volden, Ting, and Carpenter 2008). Bayesian learning does not necessarily lead to action, perhaps resulting in only a "change in one's confidence in existing beliefs" (Simmons, Dobbin, and Garrett 2006: 795) or a change of "ideas, beliefs, or values" (Heikkila and Gerlak 2013: 491). However, in research practice, "learning is *observed in actions* that are produced in response to information" (Dunlop and Radaelli 2017: 308; emphasis added). Interestingly, the Bayesian perspective also implies that the same information may lead to different outcomes for different learners if their prior beliefs were different (Gilardi 2010).

The second general approach to learning discussed widely in the state policy diffusion literature is bounded rationality, the idea that the limits of human cognition can bias learning systematically (Simon 1969). Scholars know that a comprehensive rationalist view of political behavior is incomplete (Lindblom 1959). With too many decisions to make and too much information to absorb, people develop nonobvious decision-making strategies. The vast cognitive psychology literature generated by this insight has shown that people use a variety of shortcuts and heuristics to grapple with the mass of sensory data we receive continuously (Kahneman 2011; Nisbett and Ross 1980; Weyland 2005). Policymakers are no different. For example, state legislators tend to be policy generalists with only a passing familiarity with most issues they consider (Rosenthal 2008; Squire and Moncrief 2015). At the same time, legislators are bombarded with policy information from their colleagues, lobbyists, the media, their constituents, and so forth (Krehbiel 1991; Mooney 1991).

One heuristic lawmakers may use to cope with this difficult decision-making environment is learning by analogy (Walker 1971). Caught between policy ignorance and a flood of information (Lindblom 1959), they seek lessons from similar governments addressing a similar problem. As Rose (1991: 5) said, "in policymaking circles, experience has a unique status as justification for effectiveness." For a US state, the obvious analogs are its forty-nine sister states. Analogies among states are often quite apt (Mooney 2001b). Broadly, the states have comparable histories, cultures, legal systems, and political institutions. Even Wyoming and California have much more in common than, say, Portugal and Spain. Of course, some states are more alike than are others, as will be discussed.

Heuristics like the use of analogy may help overwhelmed policymakers make decisions, but they can also bias those decisions in unexpected ways (Kahneman 2011; Weyland 2005). We acquire and use information nonrandomly, privileging certain types of evidence. For instance, confirmation bias causes people to believe more readily information that supports their predispositions than information that conflicts with them (Braman and Nelson 2007; Hinkle and Nelson n.d.; Tabor and Lodge 2006). Accessibility bias may cause states to use information from their neighboring states more than from those farther afield, regardless of its appropriateness (Iyengar 1990; Kahneman 2011). Importantly, such bias is not attenuated by simply adding more information (Butler and Pereira 2018). Thus, even if learning causes state policy diffusion, the result may not meet the normative ideal. The impact of cognitive shortcuts and heuristics on state policy diffusion is a prime area for future research. Diffusion scholars should look to the cognitive psychology literature to generate new and potentially surprising hypotheses (e.g., Kahneman 2011).

Does learning require action (Dunlop and Radaelli 2017)? As noted, a common assumption in the diffusion literature is that learning is a "process through which information is acquired, interpreted, and *acted upon*" (Mooney

2001a: 120; emphasis added). However, learning may sometimes be purely cognitive, and such "cognitive changes may not be sufficient for behavioral change" (Heikilla and Gerlak 2013: 492; see also Strebel and Widmer 2012). The scholarship on learning-based diffusion reflects the action assumption, and this focus on behavioral change undoubtedly underestimates interstate learning. This is a result both of Walker's legacy of studying policy adoption (a clear and observable act) and of the relative ease of measuring behavior rather than knowledge, values, or attitudes. As Smith (2019: 2) writes, "policy learning may facilitate the diffusion of policy, but states may learn from other states without adopting new legislation." For instance, a lawmaker might learn about the impact of a policy in another state but not believe that its benefits would outweigh the costs in their own state. The Bayesian view that learning can occur with or without action has recently gained attention among diffusion scholars (e.g., LaCombe and Boehmke 2020; Simmons, Dobbin, and Garrett 2006). In the end, Braun and Gilardi (2006: 306) provide a useful general definition of policy learning in the states: "the acquisition of new relevant information that permits the updating of beliefs about the effects of a new policy." The trick for scholars is how to assess diffusion learning empirically absent any obvious behavioral implications.

Finally, while the theoretical discussion in this literature tends to focus on micro-level learning (e.g., by lawmakers, bureaucrats, governors, etc.), its empirical assessment is done at the macro level (i.e., the states). Macro-level learning is not merely an aggregation of micro-level learning (Dunlop and Radaelli 2017; Heikkila and Gerlak 2013). How political institutions direct the flow of information and influence is one of the most general concerns of political science. Inferences about policymaker behavior from macro-level policy adoptions are open to ecological fallacy (Robinson 1950; Rose 1973). State policy diffusion scholars would be well served to understand and differentiate better between these two levels of learning in terms of each of the remaining questions in this section. As Heikkila and Gerlak (2013: 486) write, "understanding how individual learning aggregates into learning at the collective level is one of the key puzzles for scholars studying learning in collective contexts."

2.1.2 Who Learns?

Who learns in policy diffusion? Much of the state policy diffusion literature glosses over this question with the implicit assumption that "states" learn, while learning scholarship typically focuses on micro-level learning. State legislators may be the relevant learners in policy diffusion, as in the origin story of Walker

1969 (Baumgartner 2006). This seems reasonable, given US lawmakers' central role in researching and developing policy (Polsby 1975). Lawmakers' problematic decision-making environment makes their learning an interesting topic of study (Krehbiel 1991; Mooney 1991), and we know that state legislators look across state boundaries for information (Glick and Friedland 2014; Squire and Moncrief 2015).

In addition to legislators and their parent bodies, at least three other potential learners have been identified in the state policy diffusion literature. First, bureaucrats and agency heads can influence policy, and they, too, may learn from other states (Grupp and Richards 1975; Light 1978; Nicholson-Crotty and Carley 2016; Smith 2019). Bureaucrats have a different policy knowledge base than lawmakers (a deep and narrow, versus shallow and broad, understanding of policy), as well as different goals (Niskanen 1971). As such, bureaucratic learning could differ from that of legislators. Second, voters may learn about policy from other states, affecting policymaking directly through the initiative or indirectly by elected officials representing their preferences (Pacheco 2012). Finally, judicial policy diffusion among the states raises the question of how judges learn. For instance, do judges cite their neighboring states' high courts more than others' (Canon and Baum 1981; Caldiera 1985; Roch and Howard 2008)? Likewise, studies of state supreme decision-making can indirectly highlight judicial learning (Langer and Brace 2005; Patton 2007). Future scholarship should assess and differentiate the learning sources, processes, and biases of these various state political actors.

2.1.3 What Is Learned?

Next, what is learned in a policy diffusion? If learning is about information acquisition and use (Dunlop and Radaelli 2017; Krehbiel 1991), what information could policymakers glean from another government's policy experience that could be useful in their own deliberations? Crucially, the "laboratories of democracy" metaphor implies that information about a policy's *performance* elsewhere could help policymakers predict whether it would address their own problems (Volden 2006). As Rose (1991: 6) wrote, "given an authoritative policy goal, lesson-drawing seeks to use knowledge from other times and places to improve current programmes." Thus, instrumental information about a policy's impacts elsewhere may be learned, facilitating better alignment between policy outcomes and policymakers' preferences.

In addition to substantive information on policy performance, policymakers also need political information: who is for and against a proposal, and why (Shipan and Volden 2012; Simmon, Dobbins, and Garret 2006; Tein 2015)?

These are critical questions in practical state policymaking. For example, a state with divided government adopting a policy may signal to other states that it is politically safe to do so (Soule and Earl 2001). Policymakers may also learn political information from state supreme court decisions (Patton 2007) or election outcomes (Gilardi 2010).

Of course, political and policy information are not always aligned. As Bourdeaux and Chikoto (2008: 254) note, "conflicts [may] occur when policy recommendations that emerge [from policy experts] from performance reviews conflict with political pressure to protect key constituents." Thus, substantive policy information may not trump political information in state policymaking (Braun and Gilardi 2006; Karch 2007a). How policy and political information are used and interact in the diffusion process is a prime topic for future research.

What is the effect of information learned from policy adoptions elsewhere? Most state policy diffusion scholarship implicitly assumes that such lessons are positive, so that if a relevant state adopts a policy, the odds of adoption elsewhere increase. Thus, adoptions elsewhere provide affirmative lessons, the informational equivalent of the policy being successful. However, a few studies have challenged this assumption of a uniformly positive effect. Policymakers in one state may simply not like the way the policy is working elsewhere, reducing its odds of adoption (Bromley-Trujillo and Karch 2019; Karch 2006; Rose 1991; Stone 1999). Fay (2018) finds that states sometimes react to policy elsewhere by making a policy "countermove," reducing the odds of adopting of the disliked policy. Bulman-Pozen (2014) argues that "partisan federalism" may lead states controlled by the national out-party to react negatively to federal initiatives. Mooney (2001a) shows that the directional impact of adoption information can even vary over the course of a single policy diffusion. The causes and effects of negative diffusion influence merit more study.

2.1.4 Who Is Learned From?

What are the sources of learning in state policy diffusion? Certainly, a state can learn from its own experiences, especially from policies that can be easily run and evaluated in a single state, that is, "trialable" policy (Rogers 2003: 258; see also Makse and Volden 2011). Its local governments' experiences can also provide internal lessons for state policymakers (Shipan and Volden 2008). A state learning from its own post-adoption experiences can create a virtuous feedback loop of learning and improvement (Boehmke and Witmer 2004; Karch and Cravens 2014). But while state policymakers may learn from intrastate sources, these have typically been treated, at best, only as controls in state policy diffusion research, given its focus on interstate forces.

The long-emphasized source of learned information in the state policy diffusion literature is a state's peers, especially those states with which it shares a border. Walker 1969 was interested in neighboring or coregional states largely as a surrogate for other factors influencing diffusion. As Mallinson (2020b: 5) puts it, "neighboring states not only were more likely to have a similar history and culture, but they were also close enough for communications between state government officials . . . Media markets overlap, local travel is easy, elected and hired members of state government may serve in regional organizations together, and more" (see also Drolc, Ganrud, and Williams 2020). The emphasis on bordering states also fits well with the popular disease outbreak analogy, since infection requires close physical contact (Boehmke and Skinner 2012; Boushey 2010: 10–15).

On the other hand, Walker 1969 also argues that since communications and transportation have improved dramatically over the course of US history, the centrality of geographically based information sources has waned (see also Mallinson 2020b; Savage 1978). Indeed, Desmarais, Harden, and Boehmke (2015) find that most diffusion occurs among states that are *not* contiguous. Despite this argument, and decades of often conflicting empirical results (Mooney 2001a), some form of geographic-proximity independent variable remains standard in state policy diffusion models. For example, Mitchell (2018: 431) recently wrote, "diffusion through policy learning would likely exhibit a contagious effect, since a jurisdiction tends to look at its neighbors for policy ideas."

Several scholars have worked to develop more precise theory about the sources of diffused policy information. These scholars recognized that Walker 1969 used geographic proximity simply as a proxy for states' similarity with each other. As Volden (2006: 294) wrote, diffusion is "based on political, demographic, and budgetary similarities across states, rather than simple geographic proximity" (see also Bulman-Pozen 2014; Mossberger 2000; Nicholson-Crotty and Carley 2016). In particular, scholars have focused on states learning from their ideologically similar peers. Grossback, Nicholson-Crotty, and Peterson's (2004) groundbreaking paper demonstrated that including an ideological-similarity variable in a diffusion regression model can show the relationship of geographic proximity to be spurious. Carley, Nicholson-Crotty, and Miller (2017) argue that ideological peers are especially good for political information, while Mallinson (2020b) still finds that information from neighbors can reduce policy uncertainty. The sources of diffusion learning could also be influenced by how closely residents of one state relate to other states (Bricker and LaCombe 2020). The general hypothesis is that a state learns largely from similar states, not just its neighbors.

Policy diffusion could also be driven by states learning from the entire universe of previously adopting states. With modern communications and transportation and a plethora of national associations of state officials, states may learn both substantive and political lessons from the accumulation of all states' experiences with a policy. Shipan and Volden (2008: 842) call this the "opportunity to learn," hypothesizing that as more states – any states – adopt a policy, the more likely other states will be to adopt it (see also Makse and Volden 2011).[8] Taylor et al. (2012) find that when they include a state policy measure averaged nationally in their diffusion model, the regional adoption effect is no longer statistically significant. Karch et al. (2016; see also Rogers 2003: 106–18) argue that the pro-innovation bias in diffusion studies causes us to underestimate the national "opportunity to learn" influence on diffusion, while overestimating the "neighbors" effect.

Finally, certain states may serve as special role models for their peers, regardless of proximity. Walker 1969 argues that many states look for policy information and guidance from regional and national leader states. In an early follow-up, Grupp and Richards (1975) found that, indeed, certain states appear to constitute a sort of "national league" from whom many other states learn. Desmarais, Harden, and Boehmke (2015) expand on this idea by modeling influence networks in dozens of policy diffusions over the course of US history. In doing so, they estimate how much one state tends to learn from another (Gilardi, Shipan, and Wueest 2020). More work fleshing out, validating, and explaining such networks should occupy scholars for some time.

2.1.5 How Can We Observe Learning?

While defining a theoretical policy learning mechanism is challenging, its empirical assessment in state policy diffusion is even more daunting. Learning is a psychological process, and scholars in this tradition have measured it indirectly. For example, Grossback, Nicholson-Crotty, and Peterson (2004: 541) "conclude that we are observing learning" when they find that ideologically similar states are more influential on adoption than are neighboring states. Likewise, Hays (1996b: 553) claims that the existence of policy "reinvention" (see Section 3.1), the systematic modification of a policy as it diffuses, demonstrates "learning from the collective experiences of earlier adopters."

---

[8] This effect may also be due to norm-based emulation, as will be discussed.

Currently, the state-of-the-field indirect indicator of policy diffusion learning is *adoption following policy success elsewhere*. While Volden (2006: 295) develops this idea for the field, arguing that "to serve as effective policy laboratories, states must emulate only the successful policies found elsewhere," Walker (1971: 366) himself broached it decades earlier, writing that "inertia can more easily be overcome if the proponent of change can point to the successful implementation of his program in a similar setting." Elsewhere, Volden (with Shipan) writes that "the clearest evidence of learning arises when the *success* of policies helps to determine whether or not they spread from one government to another" (Shipan and Volden 2014: 360; emphasis in original). Volden, Ting, and Carpenter (2008) deduce this hypothesis formally. Conversely, Volden (2016) also shows that policy failure increases the chances of repeal elsewhere, further enhancing the external validity of a causal learning conclusion.

This "learning" variable is operationalized in a diffusion regression model as an indicator of policy success elsewhere (Nicholson-Crotty and Carley 2016; Volden 2006). Of course, this approach yields only an indirect measure of learning (Graham, Shipan, and Volden 2013), but it is theoretically justified and the current standard in the literature (Butler et al. 2017; Maggetti and Gilardi 2016; Nicholson-Crotty and Carley 2016; Volden, Ting, and Carpenter 2008). Importantly, failure to find evidence of learning in this way does not mean that no learning happened; rather, it only means that this particular form of learning from substantive or political success elsewhere did not happen. Different types of learning could drive a diffusion, and sorting these out is an important task for future research. For instance, what are the differential impacts of substantive policy learning and political learning on diffusion?

Scholars have also proposed at least two other ways to test if learning is behind a policy diffusion. Volden, Ting, and Carpenter's (2008) formal model implies that the existence of free riders in a diffusion is due to learning. Free-riding states delay adoption as they wait to learn about that policy's performance elsewhere. Scholars have also examined learning in diffusion by using state-to-state variation in legislative institutional capacity (Squire 2017). Members of well-resourced legislatures can devote more energy to policy analysis, including considering other states' experiences (LaCombe and Boehmke 2020; Shipan and Volden 2006). Thus, if professional legislatures follow policy success elsewhere more than do amateur legislatures, it suggests learning has occurred in the former. An interaction between legislative professionalism and policy success elsewhere has been used to test this hypothesis (Mossberger 2000; Shipan and Volden 2014). Similarly, Desmarais, Harden, and Boemke (2015) argue that if network connections are related to legislative professionalism, it is evidence of learning.

2.2 Competition

Learning is not the only causal mechanism by which policy ideas and information might diffuse among the states. Scholarship in economics and policy studies suggest that *competition among governments* may also lead to policy diffusion (Arel-Bundock and Parinandi 2018). A competition diffusion mechanism is fundamentally different from that of learning, with potentially distinctive causes, effects, and diffusion patterns. Thus, to understand policy diffusion, at a minimum, scholars must identify the theoretical and empirical differences between learning and competition. Some scholars have begun to do this (e.g., Baybeck, Berry, and Siegel 2011; Berry and Baybeck 2005; Boehmke and Witmer 2004), but much more work is needed.

Whereas learning is largely about the flow and use of information, *competition is about the distribution of resources* (Rom, Peterson, and Scheve 1998). This should lead to very different interactions and influences in policymaking. As Maggetti and Gilardi (2016: 91) put it, "competition occurs when units [of government] react to one another in an attempt to attract or retain resources." States compete to attract good things (tax revenue, jobs, productive residents) and repel bad things (pollution, unproductive citizens) (Karch 2007b; LaCombe and Boehmke 2020). Competition leads states to "emulate policies of other states to achieve an economic advantage ... or to avoid being disadvantaged" (Berry and Berry 2007: 225). The "driving force" behind competition-driven diffusion is mobility – of people, firms, and capital (Dye 1990: 178). Competing states adopt policies to gain advantage over their peers rather than to learn from their experiences.

While learning is typically considered sincere behavior, competition is all about strategy. Competition causes policymakers to "react to or anticipate one another in the attempt of attracting or retaining resources" (Gilardi 2016: 10; see also Shipan and Volden 2012). This strategic behavior is caused by policy externalities, that is, policy implications and impacts for states other than the one adopting it (Coates and Pearson-Merkowitz 2017). In particular, economic externalities can compel policymakers to react (Braun and Gilardi 2006; Franzese and Hays 2006; Mallinson 2020b). Policy spillovers may be positive for a nonadopting state, such as when a neighbor strengthens its clean air protections (Monogan, Konisky, and Wood 2017; Shipan and Volden 2008) or when it can sell firearms to residents of other states that have more restrictive gun control regimes (Coates and Pearson-Merkowitz 2017). However, most diffusion research on competition has considered negative externalities, such as losing tax revenue to another state or encouraging poor people to migrate (Arel-Bundock and Parinandi 2018; Berry and Berry 1990). Pacheco (2017) argues that negative externalities lead to competition among states, while positive externalities lead to free riding (see also Volden, Ting, and Carpenter 2008). Thus, negative externalities may increase the speed of a policy's diffusion, while positive externalities may actually decrease it, as the states benefiting from other states' policies simply take advantage.

A few scholars have made headway differentiating learning and competition in state policy diffusion. Berry and Baybeck (2005) hypothesize that competition depends on the distribution of the policy target in a state, while learning does not. For example, when more residents live near a border with a lottery state, their state is more likely to adopt a lottery itself to avoid losing revenue across the border (see also Baybeck, Berry, and Sigel 2011). Boehmke and Witmer (2004) also study gambling policy diffusion to tease out this distinction. They find that learning from other states tends to occur before a state's initial adoption, but once it adopts a program, that state only learns from its own experiences with it; on the other hand, economic forces behind competition persist.

Like learning, competition carries significant normative baggage. Neoliberal thinkers hold that competition among the states "creates efficiency in society as a whole, raising outputs and lowering costs" (Dye 1990: 14). The hypothesized motive is that people and firms locate to the polity that best matches their ideal policy regime (Peterson 1981; Tiebout 1956). The flow of people, firms, and capital across state borders in response to policy choices gives policymakers strong signals about constituent preferences and policy impacts. Thus, competition generates political and policy information, something that could be learned in policymaking. But the competition literature emphasizes interests, and not information flow. As Dye (1990: 189) concludes in his advocacy of competitive federalism, "the effect of competition is neither to lower nor to raise welfare spending [for example,] but to bring it into line with citizen demands." Thus, competition is hypothesized to improve representation.

On the other hand, competition may bias policymaking systematically. For instance, Thom and An (2017: 89) found that states substantially overinvested in tax credits to compete for film production "relative to their capacity to provide commensurate returns." This reflects the scholarly consensus that state tax incentives are "at most a minor factor" in firms' location decisions, and so are a waste of state resources (Woods 2006: 176; see also Turner 2003). Likewise, states may compete for business by weakening environmental regulations inordinately (Monogan, Konisky, and Woods 2017; Woods 2006, n.d.).

An extended normative argument against competition in state policy diffusion follows from the hypothesis that "a federal system will tend to provide less redistribution than if policies were set nationally" (Peterson and Rom 1989).

States competing to attract good things and repel bad things may enter into bidding wars whose logical conclusion is zero welfare benefits, business regulations, taxes, or whatever else is attracting or repelling certain populations (Leiser 2017; Woods 2006, n.d.). While one influential study supported this "race to the bottom" hypothesis for social welfare benefits (Peterson and Rom 1989), subsequent studies have found mixed evidence, at best (Berry, Fording, and Hanson 2003; Lieberman and Shaw 2000; Volden 2002). Gilardi (2016: 11) concludes that the "evidence is overwhelmingly against a uniform downward convergence" (but see Woods n.d.).

Why does interstate competition *not* cause redistributive policy to crash to zero (Arel-Bundock and Parinandi 2018)? Volden (2002) contends that inflation and strategic behavior explain the downward trend in social welfare policy, not a race to the bottom. The idea is that when inflation reduces the buying power of welfare benefits below policymakers' preferences, they wait to raise them until their neighbors do so (see also Woods 2006 on mining regulations). Thus, even without an active race to the bottom, interstate competition probably biases redistributive policy downwards. Berry, Fording, and Hanson (2003) argue that micro-level, rather than state-level, data should be used to test this mechanism since that is the level on which the motive forces work. Scholars could use microeconomic and cognitive theory to develop potentially competing hypotheses that would both further explain state policy diffusion and shed light on decision-making generally.

2.2.1 What Is Competed Over?

As with learning, the hypothesis that interstate competition influences state policymaking raises important theoretical questions. First, what is competed over? In general, states want to attract firms, labor, and capital, and they want to repel "undesirables," like pollution and poor people (Rom, Peterson, and Scheve 1998). States want to add factors of production and reduce costs (Dye 1990). This means encouraging people and firms to vote with their feet, moving to the polity with their preferred basket of policies (Peterson 1981; Tiebout 1956). States compete for firms directly through targeted tax and regulation incentives and indirectly by developing a generally "business-friendly" regulatory regime (Thom and An 2017; Turner 2003). Some policies have a "population of interest" that is relevant to competition, such as people living near a border who could easily take advantage of its neighbor's lottery or lower gasoline taxes (Berry and Baybeck 2005). States may also compete on policy substance, especially when cross-border behavior is significant. For example, in the 1970s, when the legal alcohol drinking age varied among the states, fears of teenagers driving across state lines to drink was an important part of the policy debate (Macinko and Silver 2015). Perhaps such "blood borders" will also become a talking point in the states' debates over recreational marijuana legalization (Ellison and Spohn 2017).

2.2.2 Policy Type and Competition

The emphasis in the competition literature on redistributive policy raises the question, do states compete more on some policies than others? As Shipan and Volden (2012: 790) note, on many issues, "governments have little or nothing to gain from competition." For example, perhaps states may set their education or natural resources policy with little strategic consideration of their peers' choices. As noted, states may compete on policies related to mobile factors of production (Gray 1994; Simmons, Dobbin, and Garrett 2006). To attract business and capital, states may establish favorable tax systems (Arel-Bundock and Parinandi 2018) and weak environmental regulations (Woods 2006), raising the specter of a race to the bottom. States may also compete for individuals' economic activity, such as out-of-state lottery players (Berry and Baybeck 2005; Berry and Berry 1990) or restaurant smokers (Pacheco 2017). States may also compete to repel poor people through low social welfare benefits (Berry, Fording, and Hansen 2003; Peterson and Rom 1998; Rom, Peterson, and Scheve 1998; Volden 2002). Interestingly, while most scholarship on diffusion through competition has focused on redistributive policy, Dye (1990) argues that this may be the most difficult arena for competition due to potential negative externalities. More research exploring where competition does and does not affect diffusion could provide important insights into policymakers' decision-making.

2.2.3 With Whom Do States Compete?

Next, consider with whom states compete in policymaking. Most generally, as "structurally equivalent actors" in the US federal system, states compete with other states (Burt 1987; Strang and Soule 1998). Much like the sources of policy learning, scholars have not studied this question extensively, presenting an excellent opportunity for scholars. Most published studies that have addressed this question have largely focused on bordering states. This is appropriate for studying competition due to potential cross-border policy externalities. And while this "neighbor" influence may be mitigated by better communications or transportation, this is perhaps less so than with learning. Indeed, Berry and Baybeck (2005) argue that while states can learn from any other state, competition typically occurs between neighbors. Certain policies influence the behavior of people living near state borders, such as a lottery or gasoline taxes, but other policies may lead to nationwide competition (Leiser 2017; Thom and An 2017) or competition only among a subset states (Woods 2006).

An important line of study for future scholarship could be sorting out the changes in interstate competition patterns in recent decades. For example, much as modern communications, transportation, and national professional organizations let states learn from any other state, rather than just their neighbors, the same may be true for competition. Anecdotal examples of economic development fights over plant location suggest this pattern (Turner 2003).

2.3 Emulation

Thus, scholars have worked for decades to develop causal hypotheses about how learning and competition could drive state policy diffusion. State policymakers may draw lessons from previous adopters, or they may compete to turn policy externalities to their benefit. However, early state policy diffusion scholarship – including Walker 1969 – was often ambiguous regarding causal mechanisms. Instead, these studies tended to focus simply on the *emulation* of policy across states, with little theorizing about or testing causal explanations.

These early scholars conflated competition and learning or simply equated diffusion with emulation (e.g., Crain 1966; Gray 1973a; Lutz 1987). Even some recent work has fallen prey to this (Hinkle 2015; Karch 2007b: 55). For example, Gilardi and Wasserfallen (2019: 5) write, "emulation serves ... as a residual mechanism of diffusion, encompassing research that does not assume rational and fact-based assessments of policy consequences." That is, if learning or competition does not cause diffusion, it must be just pure emulation. But the reasons behind such emulation, and even the process itself, are usually unstated. Scholars have used various labels for this residual category, such as policy transfer (Dolowitz and Marsh 1996), isomorphism (Dimaggio and Powell 1983), and convergence (Bennett 1991; Boehmke 2009b). But like the "time is ripe" non-explanation for policy adoption, these often suffer from not being falsifiable (Jacob 1988: 93).

All of this begs the question: How could emulation *cause* a policy diffusion, rather than just being an empirical regularity resulting from learning, competition, or some other process? Referring to the various hypothesized diffusion mechanisms, Maggetti and Gilardi (2016: 100) conclude that "the distance between the concept of emulation and its operationalization seems particularly vast." Walker (1971: 356) noted that "sometimes states enact legislation that is virtually copied word for word from other states," as when several states famously copied typographical errors from a 1931 California law, but he did not identify a causal mechanism for this imitation. Importantly, copying legislative language could involve a different process than copying policy ideas. For example, lawmakers may copy legislative language to reduce their workload or to avoid any unexpected consequences of modifying it, while copying ideas allows for thoughtful modification to meet local conditions. While we may observe a state copy a peer's policy, the critical theoretical question is always *why* it did so. As some diffusion scholars began to distinguish between learning and competition in the twenty-first century, others considered why one state would simply emulate the policy of another.

For theoretical guidance, scholars turned to scholarship that highlighted the power of *social norms* in small groups (Crain 1966; Dimaggio and Powell 1983; Simmons, Dobbins, and Garrett 2006). The idea is that "communities of policy experts" (Walker 1981: 79) develop policy-relevant standards, which members of those communities internalize. For example, environmental regulators tend to believe that a state's pollution regulations ought to be similar to those of its neighbors (Engel 1997). As Braun and Gilardi (2006: 310) write, "shared social-ization and repeated interactions within networks can lead to the emergence of common norms." As a result, state policymakers may feel normative pressure to achieve some national or professional standard. Thus, the motive force behind policy emulation may simply be "pride in keeping up with modern trends" (Jacob 1988: 101).

This theoretical perspective takes its cue from the definitional nuances of the words "emulation" and "imitation." The former implies an effort to meet a standard or example set elsewhere, while the latter is simply about copying and is largely agnostic about any underlying causal motivation. State policy diffusion scholars distinguish these words in this way, where copying legis-lation is an empirical regularity used as an indicator of the more theoretically interesting process of emulation (Jansa, Hansen, and Gray 2019; Kroeger 2016). Therefore, I use "emulation" in my discussion of this norm-based process.

While the development of state policymakers' associations and networks in recent decades may have enhanced policy learning (Balla 2001; Walker 1971), it could also have increased social pressure to emulate policy. Rather than policy information, policymakers tend to base their emulation decisions on "actor characteristics" (LaCombe and Boehmke 2020: 4), "copying the actions of another in order to look like that other" (Shipan and Volden 2008: 842), rather than to achieve a substantive policy goal. While learning has a fact-based frame and competition is about interests, emulation is norm-based (Gilardi, Shipan, and Wueest 2020). The causal mechanism is the urge to meet normative policy expectations, or as Shipan and Volden (2012: 791) call it, "the policy diffusion equivalent of 'keeping up with the Jones.'" Sociologists describe this as "lower ranking community members aspir[ing] to be like prestigious others" (Strang and Soule 1998: 275).

Some scholars have used emulation or copying in an epidemiological analogy for policy diffusion, modeling policy as a "contagion" that spreads through contact (Boushey 2010; Mallinson 2016). This could lead to imitation, as the contagion-policy replicates itself among the states. However, the causal mechanism behind infectious disease spread (i.e., infection by a microorganism) has no strong theoretical analog in the policy diffusion process. A theory that states emulate other states to meet shared norms is more explanatory.

2.3.1 Who Emulates?

As with learning and competition, asking several questions of the literature will help us understand emulation better. First, what types of states under what conditions adopt policy so as to meet their peers' normative expectations? Or more generally, controlling for other forces, when does norm-based emulation influence state policymaking?

Interestingly, these questions have their own normative implications, since scholars typically admire learning and object to following fashion blindly. Language in a recent article demonstrates this: "borrowing exact language might indicate *thoughtless* adherence to a political stance, *lazy* policymaking, or even *ignorance* of the exact implications of a bill's content for one's own state" (Jansa, Hansen, and Gray 2019: 741; emphases added). Emulation may provide a "quick fix" for policymakers in urgent need of a solution, but such a process "is associated with several forms of failed transfer" (Minkman, van Buuren, and Bekkers 2018: 232).

Emulation can be thought of as a cognitive strategy to cope with state policymakers' problematic information environment (Simon 1969). Thus, policymaker capacity and incentives may determine when it is used. For example, Jansa, Hansen, and Gray (2019) demonstrate that legislatures with fewer staff are more likely to copy legislative language directly from other states (see also Kroeger 2016). Term limits also reduce legislative capacity to handle substantive policy information (Kurtz, Cain, and Neimi 2007), while at the same time giving lawmakers an incentive to pass legislation quickly, given their constrained time in office (Garrett and Jansa 2015; Miller, Nicholson-Crotty, and Nicholson-Crotty 2018). Thus, states with legislative term limits and citizen legislatures may be more likely to emulate their peers' policies.

2.3.2 Who Is Emulated?

Next, consider who is emulated. The small-group literature hypothesizes that lower-ranked community members will emulate higher-ranked members (Minkman, van Buuren, and Bekkers 2018; Strang and Soule 1998), paralleling Walker's (1969) original discussion of regional and national leaders. In addition to social stratification, scholars have focused on emulation from neighboring and co-regional states, since proximity and frequent contacts can "generate pressures toward conformity" (Soule and Earl 2001: 282). Social pressures may develop among states who view themselves as peers, regardless of proximity (Butler and Pereria 2018; Grossback, Nicholson-Crotty, and Peterson 2004; Linder et al. 2020). Such homophily-oriented emulation may be based on shared political, ideological, economic, or cultural characteristics (Blau 1977). Social pressures may be based simply on the perception of similarity between a pair of states, whether by elites (Boehmke and Pacheco 2016) or voters (Bricker and LaCombe 2020; Fisher and Sloan 2018). Desmarais, Harden, and Boehmke (2015: 392) identify a complex system of "persistent policy pathways," some of which may be driven by shared norms, in addition to learning and competition.

2.3.3 What Is Emulated?

Finally, what is emulated from one state by another? Unlike with learning, where a wide variety of information could flow across state borders, emulation is all about copying legislative language (Linder et al. 2020). Emulation may also involve copying policy ideas, and future research should explore this.[9] The existing state policy diffusion literature on emulation focuses on copying legislative language. Given this, which policies are more likely to see legislative language borrowed among the states?

Highly salient and simple policies are good candidates for emulation because they (a) provide strong political motivation to act (salience), and (b) little reason to wait for policy analysis (simplicity) (Boushey 2016; Hansen and Jansa 2019; Nicholson-Crotty 2009). Divorce reform in the mid-twentieth century followed such a pattern (Jacob 1988), as did state legislative term limits in the 1990s, although the latter swept through states almost exclusively through the direct initiative process (Mooney 2009). This dynamic may lead to rapid diffusion, or a "policy outbreak" (Boushey 2010, 2016). Emulation of highly salient, low-complexity policy may be a symbolic act, making implementation and impact irrelevant (Mooney and Lee 1995). When a state chooses a policy "in order to

---

[9] Another way to think about emulation is as the result of the diffusion of social norms (Pierotti 2013).

legitimize actions, regardless of their consequences," emulation, rather than learning, is probably at work (Strebel and Widmer 2012: 389).

Swift emulation can have negative consequences, if the result is the adoption of "faddish," "inappropriate or hasty" policy (Stone 1999: 54), or "policies that are either unsuitable for their immediate problems, or worse, are outright policy failures" (Boushey 2010: 171). For example, states rapidly adopted film tax credits in the late twentieth century, only to repeal many of them when they failed to work as hoped (Thom and An 2017). Of course, a rapidly emulated program can be modified after a state learns from its own experiences with it (Karch and Cravens 2014). Emulation can be facilitated by advocacy groups promulgating model legislation, providing time- and information-strapped law-makers with well-crafted legislative language ready for introduction (Callaghan, Karch, and Kroeger 2020; Kroeger 2016). Model legislation also raises normative concerns about information asymmetry and the power of the groups that write it (Brown et al. 2019; Collingwood, El-Khatib, and O'Brien 2019; Hertel-Fernandez 2019).

Finally, emulation may be more likely in certain stages of a policy's diffusion than others. For example, learning may happen early in a diffusion, with emulation occurring only after "a threshold is reached beyond which adoption provides legitimacy rather than improves performance" (Dimaggio and Powell 1983: 52). Walker (1971: 367) plants the seed of this idea, writing that after many adoptions, a policy "may become recognized as a legitimate responsibility for all states, ... gain[ing] a momentum of its own." After policy learning yields a satisfactory understanding of a policy's effects, the "burden of proof" (Gilardi 2016: 10) switches from advocates to opponents. Once a state feels itself "relatively deprived" (Walker 1971: 386), and once the issue is "no longer a matter of broad public debate" (Finnemore and Sikkink 1988: 895), social pressure accelerates adoptions (Glick and Hays 1991). Much more theoretical development and direct testing of this norm-based emulation hypothesis are needed.

2.4 Coercion

The fourth general policy diffusion mechanism identified by scholars is coercion, when "force, threats, or incentives [are used] by one government to affect the policy decisions of another" (Shipan and Volden 2012: 791). Coercion connotes compulsion, with one government trying to impose its will on another, perhaps through a military, economic, or legal power differential between the governments in question. But coercion can range "from enforcement to gentle pressure" (Strebel and Widmer 2012: 394). While the other three diffusion mechanisms emphasize the actions of the adopter (who learns, competes, or emulates), coercion focuses on the actions and influence of an actor external to the adoption decision (Eyestone 1977; LaCombe and Boehmke 2020). Coercion occurs when "powerful actors ... impose costs and rewards on policy alternatives" under consideration by other governments (Braun and Gilardi 2006: 300). Thus, this can be a complex and subtle mechanism. Beyond direct coercion, the related, but more general, concept of the "vertical federalism" of policy across levels of government further complicates this concept, as discussed in Section 2.4.1 (Karch 2006).

Scholars of cross-national policy diffusion have examined coercion extensively, since "powerful countries can explicitly or implicitly influence the probability that weaker nations adopt the policy they prefer by manipulating the opportunities and constraints" (Simmons, Dobbins, and Garret 2006: 790). In addition to military intimidation and invasion, governments and the nongovernmental organizations they work through can exercise "soft coercion" through incentives and nudges (Simmons, Dobbins, and Garret 2006: 791). For instance, the World Bank often requires recipient governments to make specific policy changes as a condition of aid (Chiuri, Ferri, and Majnoni 2001). While a potential recipient of aid is not forced to accept such policy changes, as might be the case following a military invasion, the imbalance of power can influence policymaking. Scholars of state policy diffusion have not considered interstate coercion as a cause of policy adoption. While the power differential among the states may be insufficient for coercion today, with continued economic polarization in the USA, it may occur in the future.

2.4.1 Vertical Federalism

For US state policy diffusion scholars, discussion of coercion focuses on federalism, especially "vertical federalism," where one level of government influences the policies of another level, whether through coercion or some other mechanism (Karch 2006; Karch and Rosenthal 2016; Shipan and Volden 2006). To this point in this essay, I have focused on horizontal federalism, with state governments influencing their peers. The normative "laboratories of democracy" argument implies one dimension of vertical federalism, with the federal government learning from the states (Karch and Rosenthal 2016; Lieberman and Shaw 2000; Mossberger 1999). This is not coercion, of course, since a state may not compel or even incentivize federal policymaking in any meaningful way.

The US Constitution defines the relationships among the local, state, and federal governments. The state–local constitutional relationship is straightforward: local governments are fully creatures of the state, with no independent authority (Gillette 1991). As such, states can diffuse policy among their local governments simply by legislative fiat (Kim, McDonald, and Lee 2018; Shipan and Volden 2006; Zimmerman 1976). Political considerations may attenuate states' propensity to impose local mandates, but their constitutional authority is clear. Recent state-level efforts to preempt local government policy on minimum wage, pandemic mask wearing, and immigration might be thought of as "negative diffusion" (Bromley-Trujillo and Karch 2020; Mooney 2001a; Soule and Earl 2001; Strang and Tuma 1993), that is, as a backlash to enacted or proposed local policy.

Coercion in state policy diffusion is far more interesting when considering the more ambiguous power relationship between the federal and state governments (Jensen 2016). As the 10th Amendment states: "The powers not delegated to the United States by the Constitution, nor prohibited by it to the States, are reserved to the States respectively, or to the people." Thus, for most domestic policy, the federal government cannot simply force a state to adopt a policy, as the states can do with their locals.

During the Great Depression of the 1930s, the Roosevelt administration sought to influence state social welfare policy, but it was blocked from direct coercion by the US Supreme Court's interpretation of the 10th Amendment (Carson and Kleinerman 2002). Instead, the federal government leveraged its tremendous revenue-generating power by offering states *financial incentives* to adopt specified policies voluntarily, a process dubbed "fiscal federalism" (Wallis and Oates 1998; Welch and Thompson 1980). Fiscal federalism is not pure coercion, since states are largely sovereign on domestic issues, but with large incentives, federal pressure may be difficult to resist. For example, in the 1980s, the federal government leveraged its 90 percent match on highway construction funds to incentivize states to adopt a twenty-one-year-old minimum drinking age for alcohol (Macinko and Silver 2015; Shipan and Volden 2006). More recently, Medicaid expansion under Obamacare caused consternation among state policymakers who were philosophically opposed to the policy but who still found it hard to pass up such federal largess (Barrilleaux and Rainey 2014; Rigby 2012). Today, fiscal federalism is an integral part of the US federal domestic agenda, from transportation to public health to social welfare policy. Since incentives are a less precise form of coercion than a mandate, establishing effective incentive regimes is challenging. For example, the 1996 federal welfare reforms included a variety of incentives for state policy change, and the states responded to them heterogeneously (Filindra 2013; Soss et al. 2001).

Something like coercion – perhaps intimidation? – may also be effected simply by a legally, economically, or socially powerful government signaling its preferences (Allen, Pettus, and Haider-Markel 2004; Goggin et al. 1990). Karch (2006: 403) argues that federal government signals can affect state choices "by altering the strength of the obstacles that prevent innovation or by providing resources to help overcome these obstacles." In particular, "credible, clear, consistent, repeated and received" (Hannah and Mallinson 2018: 404) signals from the national government may influence states' policy decisions even in the absence of incentives. For example, congressional hearings can send signals to state policymakers, even when not resulting in legislation (Karch 2012; Karch and Rosenthal 2016). Discussion in Washington gives state policymakers both policy and political information. While this could facilitate policy learning, it could also lead to strategic responses by state policymakers to potential federal action (McCann, Shipan, and Volden 2015). Sorting out this complex relationship is an important task for researchers.

US Supreme Court decisions send both binding and nonbinding policy signals to the states, defining the "constitutional context" of state policymaking (Patton 2007). While federal judicial review of state law can have direct and compulsory impacts on state policy (e.g., Baker 1966), court decisions on peripheral issues, certiorari choices, and other tangential signals can also influence state policymaking (Gleason and Howard 2014; Hinkle 2015).

What impact does federal coercion – hard or soft – have on state policy diffusion? First, federal incentives speed up policy diffusion (Boushey 2012; Gray 1973a; Welch and Thompson 1980), but scholars have also found subtler effects. For example, Karch (2007a) hypothesizes a "percolation effect," a reciprocal relationship where early adopting states demonstrate the policy's value to national leaders, who, in turn, encourage its adoption in other states through incentives, signals, or mandates. McCann, Shipan, and Volden (2015: 496) suggest that professional legislatures are more likely to "seize upon the policy solutions entertained at the national level and advance them in their home states," allowing well-resourced and ambitious lawmakers to champion popular programs. Similarly, Shipan and Volden (2006) distinguish between a "snowball effect" and a "safety-value effect" (see also Karch and Rosenthal 2016). Well-resourced state policymakers may use federal signals as extra support for their interests at home (snowball effect), while less-resourced policymakers may use federal action as an excuse to ignore the issue (pressure value effect). Heterogeneous effects may mask each other, biasing research results against finding true relationships, thus increasing Type II error.

Finally, scholars have begun trying to explain cases where a state bucks federal incentives and signals (Callaghan, Karch, and Kroeger 2020). For example, Hannah and Mallinson (2018) ask why a state would pass "defiant" medical marijuana policy in the face of a clear negative signal from the federal government. They find that "federal signals appear to have had little impact on defiant adoption" (Hannah and Mallinson 2018: 414), suggesting a limit to federal power. Furthermore, Bulman-Pozen (2014) argues that the federal structure of US political parties gives the national out-party the incentive and opportunity to fight against national policy in the state governments it controls. The politics of the Affordable Care Act demonstrated this, with many GOP-led states refusing massive federal incentives to implement it (Rigby 2012). This counterintuitive rejection of federal funds has occurred with other diffusions as states try to control their own policy agendas, and the reasons for this surprising behavior need more research (Arsneault 2001; Barrilleaux and Rainey 2014; Kincaid 2017; Nicholson-Crotty 2012).

2.5 The Contingency of Diffusion Mechanisms and Causal Factors

So far, I have discussed the hypothesized causal mechanisms behind diffusion largely as distinct forces potentially at work in a state policy diffusion. In this section, I discuss the literature on how the effects of these mechanisms might be contingent, based on various dimensions.

First, characteristics of the policy under consideration may influence which mechanism is at work in its diffusion. For example, complex policy may diffuse with more or less learning than does simpler policy (Makse and Volden 2011; Nicholson-Crotty 2009). While there is much to learn about such policies, their very complexity may overwhelm policymakers, leading them to eschew substantive learning in favor of simpler emulation. Complexity and salience may interact, with highly salient and simple policies diffusing faster (Mallinson 2020a) and with more learning (Thom and An 2017) than other types of policy. "Trialability," or the ability to conduct trial and error learning on an adopted policy, may encourage states to learn from their own experiences rather than those of others (Rogers 2003: 258). Constitutional amendment and statute adoption may be driven by different diffusion mechanisms (Fay and Wegner 2016).

The effectiveness of diffusion mechanisms may change over the course of a policy's diffusion. Walker (1971: 367) raised this issue, writing that at a certain point in its diffusion, a policy "may become recognized as a legitimate responsibility for all states." So while early adoptions may be motivated by competition or learning, normative emulation may be more frequent for later adoptions, precisely as Mallinson 2020a finds (see also DiMaggio and Powell 1983; Strang and Soule 1998). Leiser (2017) finds a complementary pattern: regional effects fade as a diffusion progresses. Bouche and Volden (2011) find that competition initially drove foster care privatization, while learning was more important for later adopters. More theory and testing are needed here.

The use of diffusion mechanisms may vary across policymaking phases. Most state policy diffusion research has focused on the adoption phase, but some scholars have recently expanded their analyses. For example, the first thing that must diffuse among the states is the idea of the policy itself (Gilardi, Shipan, and Wueest 2020), and the imagery, interpretation, and branding of a policy may also diffuse in the policy development phase (Strang and Soule 1998; Tolbert and Zucker 1983). Problem definition and framing depend critically on the flow of information within and among the states (Boushey 2016; Lowery, Gray, and Baumgartner 2010). Agenda setting has been studied using bill introductions (Bromley-Trullijo and Karch 2020), and scholars have looked at the influences on post-adoption modification and amendment (Boehmke and Witmer 2004; Karch and Cravens 2014). Several studies show how the influences on these phases differ, sometimes implying distinct causal mechanisms. For example, state neighbor-to-neighbor diffusion is more likely in agenda setting than in adoption (Mintrom 1997). Boehmke and Witmer (2004) find that while states may learn from other states for initial adoption, they learn from their own experiences as they subsequently amend and update the policy after adoption.

In addition to the contingency of mechanisms, recent studies have also explored the contingency of the various influences on diffusion. For example, when compared with citizen legislatures (Squire 2017), professional legislatures learn more from other states (Shipan and Volden 2012, 2014) and respond more quickly to congressional activity and strong advocates (McCann, Shipan, and Volden 2015). Likewise, term-limited legislatures are less likely to learn from their neighbors (Miller, Nicholson-Crotty, and Nicholson-Crotty 2018). Parinandi (2013) finds that well-resourced bureaucracies with significant discretion can speed up diffusion, and Pacheco (2013) shows that public opinion's influence on state policy adoption is contingent on legislative professionalism and policy salience. Finally, Karch (2007a) shows that legislative time constraints are most important during adoption, but political factors matter more in later phases (see also Carley, Nicholson-Crotty, and Miller 2017).

Clearly, the contingency of diffusion mechanisms and causal factors is an important area for future research. Just as the past generation of scholars has developed Walker's question from *whether* policies diffuse to *how* they diffuse, scholars now need to develop the question of *when* they diffuse. Teasing out these contingencies could deepen our understanding of diffusion and policymaking in many ways.

3 Beyond Mechanisms: Other Questions of State Policy Diffusion

The fecundity of Walker 1969 has been such that, in addition to generating a wide range of theoretically interesting questions about diffusion mechanisms, it has inspired several other important lines of scholarship related to state policy diffusion.

3.1 Reinvention

"Policy reinvention" refers to how a policy's content is modified systematically over the course of its diffusion. In one of the first state policy reinvention studies, Clark (1985: 63) noted that "the underlying assumption of the diffusion research perspective seems to be that all states adopt exactly the same policy," a strong and empirically dubious assumption. Indeed, since policies are often "complex, with varying scopes and multiple components" (Taylor et al. 2012: 78), they rarely diffuse in identical language – or even with identical intent. Walker (1973: 1190) wondered whether during a diffusion "proposals [are] so thoroughly modified that they are actually different bills," raising both methodological and theoretical concerns (Linder et al. 2020). During a diffusion, policymakers and advocates voice their opinions and push their agendas in multiple venues, often leading to amendments to the proposed legislation (Baumgartner and Jones 1993; Glick and Hays 1991; Kingdon 1995). Sometimes a state borrows "little more than a 'policy label' and a general concept" (Mossberger 2000: 191). Even the popular "no-fault divorce" reforms of the mid-twentieth century were quite heterogeneous (Jacob 1988). While policy labels and general similarities are important, legislative language directly affects a policy's outcomes and politics.

The central hypothesis of the existing reinvention literature is that *later adopters implement more extensive and comprehensive policy than those adopting early* (Allen and Clark 1981; Clark and French 1984; Hays 1996a, 1996b). The idea is that "policymakers' risk aversion and tendency toward incremental policymaking suggest that early adopters' experiences might provide administrative or political lessons that enable later adopters to expand on their efforts" (Karch 2007b: 70). For example, if North Dakota increases its highway speed limit from sixty-five to seventy miles per hour with no ill effects, neighboring Montana might then raise its limit from sixty-five to seventy-five miles per hour with approximately the same relative risk. This comprehensiveness hypothesis is based on the "anchoring" decision-making heuristic, giving decision-makers a model to follow and the incentive not to get too far ahead of it (Kahneman 2011: 119–28; Rogers 2003: 180–88; Weyland 2005).

Reinvention allows policymakers to adapt a policy to their unique circumstances, perhaps with some anchoring bias (Gilardi and Wasserfallen 2019;

Jansa, Hansen, and Gray 2019; Minkman, van Buuren, and Bekkers 2018; Rose 1991). As Berry and Berry (2017: 283) write, "implicit in the notion of reinvention is an assumption that learning is the mechanism for diffusion," highlighting reinvention's normative overtones. Ironically, the comprehensiveness hypothesis implies that, since later-adopting states learn from early adopters, diffusion laggard states may end up with even more comprehensive policy than do leaders (Mooney and Lee 1995).

Beyond reinvention during adoption, a state may modify a policy after its passage through new legislation or even a complete repeal (Thom and An 2017; Volden 2016). While little scholarship has distinguished between reinvention and modification (but see Karch 2007a, 2007b; Karch and Cravens 2014), they may be distinct processes. Before adopting a policy, the most relevant information available to a state's policymakers is from peer states that have already adopted it. But once a state adopts some form of the policy, it has direct information from its own experience to guide subsequent modifications (Boehmke and Witmer 2004; Carley, Nicolson-Crotty, and Miller 2017). Scholars should explore how this distinction can be exploited theoretically and empirically.

Recently, Parinandi (2020) broached the question of true invention – why would a state be the *first* to adopt a policy? Given the potentially idiosyncratic nature of invention, diffusion scholars have self-consciously avoided this question. But Parinandi finds a theoretically interesting pattern of invention, with more liberal state legislatures more likely to invent, and legislatures with more politically vulnerable members more likely to borrow. Given the importance of agenda setting in policymaking (Bachrach and Baratz 1962; Baumgartner and Jones 1993; Weyland 2005), more research needs to be done here.

The literature on which states reinvent what policy from which other states largely parallels the literature on diffusion mechanisms. For example, low-resourced legislatures, whether from a lack of staff or term limits, reinvent less and copy more (Jansa, Hansen, and Gray 2019; Hansen and Jansa 2019; Hays 1996a; Kroeger 2016). Professional legislatures are better able to evaluate and adjust policy to local conditions, while citizen legislatures are more likely to copy their peers' legislative language and hope for the best. Examining the sources of policy information and influence, Carley, Nicholson-Crotty, and Miller (2017) find that states look to their neighbors for adoption, their ideological peers for reinvention, and their own experiences for post-adoption modification. More research is needed to verify and explain this intriguing pattern. What policies are more likely to be reinvented as they diffuse? Hansen and Jansa (2019) find that complex policies exhibit frequent reinvention, but this may be due to something inherent in complexity or just more opportunities to make changes. Mooney and Lee (1995, 1999) find that even relatively simple morality policy can be reinvented systematically, supporting the comprehensiveness hypothesis. Finally, national interest groups can develop model legislation to assist their advocacy, with at least one such group "tak[ing] great care in designing model legislation that is easily adaptable across states" (Brown et al. 2019: 10; see also Hertel-Fernandez 2019). And the more adaptable a policy is to local conditions, the quicker it will diffuse (Levi-Faur 2015). Thus, sophisticated advocates use reinvention strategically.

Beyond comprehensiveness, reinvention may proceed in multiple directions, based on the states' heterogeneous interests and preferences (Glick and Hays 1991). The progressive comprehensiveness hypothesis is based on the assumption of rational learning and common interests among states, both of which can be problematic. Different interests could lead to different reinvention streams for a policy, a hypothesis needing further development and testing. Parinandi (2020) and Kreitzer and Boehmke (2016) demonstrate how to differentiate such divergent streams. Beyond this, post-adoption modification by early adopters may negate any "comprehensiveness" differential as the diffusion progresses, since early and late adopters can both learn from experience, continually adjusting policy to meet their needs (Hays 1996b). Many interesting theoretical questions remain to be addressed about policy reinvention.

3.2 Diffusion Across Time

While state policy diffusion scholarship has primarily focused on how policies spread geographically (e.g., Walker's "spreading ink-blots on a map" [1971: 1187]), thinking about how diffusion proceeds over time has also contributed to our understanding of policymaking (Mooney and Lee 1995). Indeed, Walker (1973: 1186–87) stated that "the central problem I dealt with [in Walker 1969] involved the relative speed with which states adopted new ideas," a temporal issue. "Relative speed" was used to assess which states were most innovative (see Section 3.2.1). Another temporal dimension that has been leveraged for theoretical and empirical benefit is the speed at which policies diffuse across the states (Graham, Shipan, and Volden 2012). Some policies move through the states slowly and methodically (e.g., see Jacob 1988 on no-fault divorce), while others sweep through the country quickly (e.g., see Boushey 2010 on Amber Alert Laws). What explains variation in these temporal dimensions?

First, Walker 1969 and Gray 1973a suggested that diffusion processes and relationships may have changed in the decades covered by Walker's diffusion dataset. Indeed, the fact that a diffusion may take many years or decades to run its course makes a changing political and substantive context an ongoing concern. Improvements in communication and transportation, changes in political institutions, and the development of national professional organizations for state officials in the late twentieth century probably have affected diffusion in many ways, including reinvention, which scholars are just beginning to explore (e.g., Boehmke et al. 2020; Drolc, Gandrud, and Williams 2020; Mallinson 2020b; Miller, Nicholson-Crotty, and Nicholson-Crotty 2018).

An ongoing challenge for scholars of temporal diffusion phenomena has been to avoid confounding units of analysis, as reflected in the questions previously mentioned. Critiques of Walker 1969's state innovativeness scores (e.g., Eyestone 1977; Gray 1973a; Levi-Faur 2015; Rose 1973) can seem confusing and contradictory until one differentiates between the "speed" of the policy diffusion itself (that is, how quickly a policy spreads across the country) and the "innovativeness" of a state (that is, how likely a state is to adopt a new policy). The appropriate units of analysis here are the policy diffusion and the state, respectively, with each phenomenon having an important temporal dimension. Walker 1969 focuses on state innovativeness, the subject of most subsequent time-based diffusion scholarship (e.g., Boehmke and Skinner 2012; Savage 1978), but the speed of a policy's diffusion has also been studied (e.g., Boushey 2010, 2012; Gray 1973a; Mallinson 2016; Nicholson-Crotty 2009).

3.2.1 State Innovativeness

Walker 1969's "central question" – why are some states more innovative than others? – is a temporal issue because it involves arranging states in the order of their adoption of a given policy. If a state is an early adopter consistently over several policies, Walker inferred that it is more "innovative" than a state that tends to adopt policy after many of its peers do. Scholars have tried to explain innovativeness by identifying traits that "make [states] significantly more or less susceptible to emerging innovations" (Boushey 2010: 136). Hypotheses about innovativeness arise both from the popular notion that some states are national policy leaders and from Walker 1969's original diffusion data, which lend support to this notion.

What does it mean for a state to be "innovative?" Early thinking followed the observation that certain states are often in the policy vanguard, while others more typically lag behind their peers. By definition, there will always be earlier and later adopters of a policy; the question is whether there is a *general tendency* to be innovative relative to other states" (Foster 1978: 180; emphasis added). Furthermore, Desmarais, Harden, and Boehmke (2015) recently posed the theoretically and methodologically provocative question of, rather than simply adopting early, if a state is more innovative when its adoption leads other states to adopt, explicitly tapping into the leadership frame. Scholars must better define the concept of state innovativeness, including whether it exists at all.

As elsewhere in the state policy diffusion literature, the concept of policy innovativeness has a normative connotation: innovation is good. For instance, Gray (1974) equates innovativeness with "progressivism," another value-laden word. Through this normative lens, being innovative seems equivalent to being better, more up-to-date, and more modern. States that regularly adopt new policies earlier than other states are deemed "innovative," being "leaders" rather than "laggards," with the attendant normative connotations thereof (Rogers 2003: 283; Rose 1991; Stone 1999; Walker 1969).

Most scholarship on state innovativeness has followed Walker 1969's general methodological path, with additional data and some statistical adjustments (Boehmke and Skinner 2012; Boushey 2010; Foster 1978; Savage 1978). First, a large set of policy diffusions is captured, where for each diffusion, the raw data consist of the states ordered sequentially by their adoption dates for that policy. Walker 1969 used 88 diffusions, Savage 1978 increased this to 181 diffusions, and Boehmke and Skinner 2012 used 189. Most ambitiously, Boehmke et al. (2020) have recently published 728 diffusions in the publically available State Policy Innovation and Diffusion (SPID) database. Second, for each diffusion, the proportion of the total length of time between the policy's first adoption and the current adoption is calculated. For instance, if Policy X diffused among the fifty states in one hundred years, and if State A adopted it seventy-five years after the first adoption, State A would have taken 75 percent of the total diffusion time to adopt. Third, these scores on the various diffusions are combined for each state, yielding its average innovativeness score. Scholars have improved this approach incrementally, most recently with Boehmke and Skinner's (2012) development of time-varying measures.

If policy innovativeness is a valid state-level concept, a question arises: what could cause a state to be more or less innovative? Walker 1969 famously argues that states with more "slack resources" are more innovative. Wealthy states can try a new policy with less-dire financial risk than poor states. States with major urban centers and a large, well-educated population are regularly exposed to new ideas, an important resource in policymaking. Walker's findings that a state's wealth, population, urbanization, and education levels are associated with innovativeness "remain among the most replicated and robust findings in policy diffusion research" (Boushey 2010: 94). Legislative capacity, in terms of both professionalism and the lack of term limits, may also enhance innovativeness, although empirical results have been mixed (Boehmke and Skinner 2012; Boushey 2010; Miller, Nicholson-Crotty, and Nicholson-Crotty 2018; Walker 1971). In the tradition of the "SES vs political institutions" state expenditure literature of the 1960s (see Section 1.1), Walker 1969 also tested the effects of party competition and malapportionment on innovativeness, but neither he nor subsequent scholars got much empirical traction here. Boushey (2010) has had some success assessing the impacts of state political ideology and culture on innovativeness.

Walker 1969's take on innovativeness generated some of the earliest controversies in the state policy diffusion literature, especially Gray's (1973b) well-known critique (see also Eyestone 1977; Rose 1973). First, scholars debate the very existence of a state policy innovativeness trait, since it is not obvious that there is any "*general proclivity* of a state to innovate across a wide range of issue areas" (Berry and Berry 2007: 233; emphasis in the original). Even if innovativeness does vary among the states at a given moment, a policy may take decades to diffuse fully, so aggregating across time and policy, as Walker 1969 does, likely reduces the precision of any innovativeness measure (Boehmke and Skinner 2012; Mallinson 2016; Nicholson-Crotty 2009; Savage 1978). Gray argued that diffusion heterogeneity both causes serious measurement issues and calls into question the very concept of innovativeness. She concluded that "'innovativeness' is not a pervasive factor; rather, it is issue- and time-specific at best" (Gray 1973a: 1185). Walker (1973: 1189) agreed, concluding that "it is very likely that 'innovativeness' is an impermanent condition, and that periods of pioneering innovation by a state government often are followed by periods of consolidation."

If a state's propensity to adopt a policy is contingent on other factors, it further challenges the notion of a general innovativeness trait (Glick and Hays 1991). For example, policy complexity and salience may cause state innovativeness scores to vary among the states (Mallinson 2016; Nicholson-Crotty 2009). Lutz (1997) finds that states leading in judicial innovation are not the same states that Walker found to be legislative leaders (but see Caldeira 1985). On the other hand, several studies have found reliable patterns of innovativeness, at least for some states and time periods (e.g., Boehmke and Skinner 2012; Freeman 1985; Foster 1978; Savage 1978). This question continues to inspire scholars, with major advances in the last decade. For instance, Boushey (2010) examines innovativeness in two different types of diffusion (incremental learning and policy breakouts), while Boehmke and Skinner (2012) address some statistical concerns with the measure, such as right censoring and over-time variation. Whether a consistent state policy innovativeness trait exists remains an open question.

3.2.2 Policy Speed

Switching the unit of analysis from the state to the policy diffusion, the heterogeneity of diffusion processes raises two other temporal issues in this literature – variation in diffusion speed over the course of a single policy diffusion and variation in diffusion speed among policies. First, consider how policies might diffuse at different rates.

Some policies diffuse to all states within a decade, while some take a century or more to do so; many policies are never adopted by every state (Boehmke et al. 2020). Scholars have typically explained this variation in diffusion speed using policy characteristics. For example, policies backed by federal incentives tend to diffuse faster (Gray 1973a; Mallinson 2016; Welch and Thompson 1980). Rogers (2003: 229–65) identifies five innovation characteristics that can influence diffusion speed – relative advantage, compatibility, trialability, observability, and complexity. State policy diffusion scholars have not examined these factors extensively, except for complexity, which has been shown to slow diffusion, especially if a learning mechanism is at work (Mallinson 2016; Nicholson-Crotty 2009). Controversy may also slow a policy's diffusion (Crain 1966). Pacheco (2017) finds that when competition drives a diffusion, the externalities involved can influence its speed. Boushey (2012) argues that if a policy's target population reflects accepted stereotypes, it diffuses faster.

A policy's salience may also affect its diffusion speed. Punctuated equilibrium theory suggests that highly salient policies are prone to "breakouts," where a policy diffuses faster than with the incremental learning typical of nonsalient policy (Baumgartner and Jones 1993; Boushey 2010). Of course, any impact of salience must surely be conditioned on public opinion. A salient and well-loved policy may be adopted quickly, while a salient and hated policy may not. These studies suggest that pooling policies with different levels of public support into a single analysis can bias salience's estimated impact on diffusion speed toward zero (Mallinson 2016). Even within a single substantive policy category, heterogeneity on complexity, saliency, and environmental factors have led Boushey (2010: 134) to reject the hypothesis that diffusion speed is "stable across policy types."

3.2.3 The S-shaped Curve

Continuing with a policy diffusion as the unit of analysis, another question is: Does speed change during a single diffusion? That is, is a policy adopted at systematically different rates over the course of its diffusion, and if so, what does that tell us about policymaking? One such pattern of rate change holds a long and honored place in the diffusion literature – the S-shaped curve of cumulative adoptions over time (Gray 1973a; Mooney and Lee 1995; Rogers 2003: 272–75). As Tarde (1903: 127) wrote in one of the earliest diffusion studies in sociology, this pattern means that a diffusion proceeds with "a slow advance in the beginning, followed by rapid and uniformly accelerated pace, followed again by progress that continues to slacken until it finally stops." Other states are cautious as a few pioneering states try something new. Once information about the policy's performance is available – and if it is successful – a rush of adoptions follows, followed by the last few "laggards" adopting begrudgingly at the end. Likewise, Weyland's (2005: 265) qualitative analysis leads him to talk of diffusion "waves – starting slowly, then gathering speed, and eventually tapering off."

What might the S-shaped curve suggest about policymaking and diffusion mechanisms? Karch and Cravens (2014: 465) argue that "the S-shaped curve is generally associated with an incremental learning process," with most states waiting and watching while a few leaders experiment with a policy. Rogers (2003: 272) believes that this pattern suggests incremental learning early in a diffusion, followed by norm-based emulation. Mallinson (2020a) also argues that changes in speed over the course of a diffusion indicate multiple causal mechanisms, with different factors influencing adoption at different stages of a diffusion.

There is debate about whether the S-shaped curve exists and, if so, what it means substantively. While Gray (1973a) claims that this curve is based on the cumulative normal distribution, Berry and Berry (2007: 241; emphasis in original) remind us that "this S-curve will result from *any* process that produces a period of more frequent adoptions (which is inevitably followed by a tapering off in the rate of adoptions as the number of remaining potential adopters declines)." Rogers (2003: 272) seems to accept the normality of policy diffusion, not from any evidence or substantive theory, but simply because of the general belief that "many human traits are normally distributed." Along with this weak theoretical justification, a practical problem for scholars is that, while the S-shaped curve is very easy to "see" in a cumulative plot of adoptions, it is hard to *test* statistically (e.g., Carley, Nicholson-Crotty, and Miller 2017; Gray 1973a; Macinko and Silver 2015; Meseguer 2006; Mooney and Lee 1995). Admirably, Boushey (2010: 53–55) moves beyond the eyeball test, applying statistical tests to the distribution of adoption rates. However, such tests have low statistical power (Ghasemi and Zahediasl 2012), further biasing conclusions toward accepting the S-shaped curve hypothesis too easily.

Rogers (2003: 277) writes that "the S-curve of diffusion is so ubiquitous that students of diffusion often expect every innovation to be adopted over time in an S-shaped pattern," but the exact functional form of the distribution "ought to be regarded as an open question." Several examples of individual policy diffusions are found in the literature that do not follow the S-shaped curve, even with a generous eyeball test (Boushey 2010; Crain 1966; Glick and Hays 1991; Gray

1973a; Hays and Glick 1997; Macinko and Silver 2015; Mallinson 2016). Mallinson (2020a) finds that cumulative state policy diffusion distributions may have fatter tails and narrower shoulders than a normal distribution, suggesting that there are more leaders and laggards than previously expected. Whether policy diffusions share a common underlying cumulative frequency distribution, what shape that distribution takes, and what substantive meaning that distribution has for state policy diffusion remain important open questions. We need both better theory and better tests to determine whether the S-shaped curve, so frequently discussed in this literature, represents an informative substantive phenomenon or is simply an artifact of the Central Limit Theorem.

3.3 External Vectors of Diffusion

How does policy and political information spread around the country, and how does this affect state policy diffusion? Boushey (2010) makes an important contribution here by highlighting the "vectors," or pathways, of transmission in his epidemiological model of diffusion. Just as school children, academic conferences, and choir practices can be vectors of disease, scholars have studied the actors and processes involved in the transmission of policy-relevant information to understand their impact on policy diffusion.

One vector of information flow is the mass media, with "time-pressed officials from across the ideological spectrum rely[ing] on centralized sources of information, such as national media coverage, in deciding which issues to address" (Bromley-Trujillo and Karch 2020: 2; see also Strang and Soule 1998). Indeed, this may beg the question of whether state policy diffusion is merely an epiphenomenon of the nationalization of the US mass media. A body of information shared nationally by policymakers could encourage policy diffusion among the states, regardless of mechanism, but the details of any such effect need to be fleshed out both empirically and theoretically. Scholars need to consider both independent and conditional effects of the media on state policy diffusion. Multi-state media markets provide excellent empirical leverage for such research (Berry and Baybeck 2005; Pacheco 2012).

While the media usually do not advocate for policy, other information vectors in the policymaking process act more intentionally and strategically in this respect. These are what Walker (1981: 77) called "prime-moving organizations," whose goal is to influence policy. Scholars have long noted the important role of "go-betweens," "boundary spanners," and "policy brokers" in diffusion, those people and groups who move information strategically from one policymaking setting to another (Graham, Shipan, and Volden 2013; Heikkila and Gerlak 2013; Pierotti 2013). Most generally, Rose (1991:

15–16) discusses "epistemic communities," or informal networks of people "with a claim to policy-relevant knowledge based upon common professional beliefs and standards of judgment, and common policy concerns" (see also Fisher and Sloan 2018; Simmons, Dobbins, and Garret 2006). Members of such communities could be lawmakers, bureaucrats, lobbyists, and other advocates, with their informal roles and relationships potentially being as important in policymaking as their formal ones (Granovetter 1973; Minkman, van Buuren, and Bekkers 2018). Epistemic community members may have diverse and intense opinions on a given policy option (Rose 1991). For example, a labor economist working for the AFL-CIO and one working for the Chamber of Commerce may share an epistemic community, based on their education, training, and experiences, but they likely have very different opinions on labor policy. While members of an epistemic community may hold different policy opinions, they share policy expertise, intense interest, and a long-run perspective on a given issue.

Epistemic communities may also be developed through practical connections, like shared conferences, publications, formal education, and professional networks (Dimaggio and Powell 1983; Rose 1991; Walker 1981). Membership in an epistemic community "helps build common norms" and can act as "an agent of socialization" for new and aspiring members (Braun and Gilardi 2006: 310). Members of these communities may develop a "seemingly disinterested and objective analysis" of policy options (Simmons, Dobbins, and Garret 2006: 800), an analysis that other members may then use in advocacy. Thus, epistemic community members often provide nonexpert policymakers with information that has the patina of science and objectivity, enhancing its credibility (Collingwood, El-Khatib, and O'Brien 2019). These communities may have "a set of agreed doctrines or theories that may be regarded as a paradigm" on a given public problem, and "peer-group approval" can then influence policy decisions (Walker 1981: 80). The policy information and norms shared by these communities relate directly to learning and emulation, respectively.

Beyond this nebulous notion of "epistemic communities," who intentionally transports policy-relevant information across state lines? The state policy diffusion literature examines at some length the influence of two such external vectors: interest groups and policy entrepreneurs.

3.3.1 Interest Groups

National interest groups can develop and transmit highly technical and even proprietary information on an issue (Walker 1991). When group members share interests across the states, pooling resources nationally can enhance their research and knowledge bases significantly, especially developing and transmitting information about policy effectiveness in the various states. According to Garrett and Jansa (2015: 392), "interest groups bolster the network by providing technical, legal, and political information." Interest groups tend to be narrowly focused and gain influence through a monopoly on technical information and targeted political clout (Nownes 2012), but advocates of popular programs may also succeed simply by spreading the word broadly, hoping for quick emulation. For example, women's groups helped spread mothers' pensions programs across the states rapidly – even before US women had the right to vote (Skocpol et al. 1993). Likewise, the group, US Term Limits, helped twenty-one states adopt legislative term limits in less than a decade (Mooney 2009). The strength of relevant interest groups is often found to be correlated with policy adoption in this literature (e.g., Karch and Rosenthal 2016; Mintrom 1997; Shipan and Volden 2012).

Recently, scholars have begun to study an interest group tactic with special relevance to state policy diffusion – model legislation (Brown et al. 2019; Collingwood, El-Khatib, and O'Brien 2019; Garret and Jansa 2015; Hertel-Fernandez 2019; Kroeger 2016). Model legislation is legal language that a group wants to be enacted, providing busy lawmakers both policy information and a specific, actionable proposal (Stein 2013). National interest groups typically have more resources to do this than their state-level affiliates, and they typically have a greater interest on a given issue than virtually any lawmaker. Writing model legislation lets a group define the problem and solution, effectively setting the agenda on the issue. Scholars have used plagiarism-detection software to trace how model legislation language diffuses through the states (e.g., Callaghan, Karch, and Kroeger 2020; Kroeger 2016).

Garret and Jansa (2015: 388) argue that "interest groups, rather than innovative and early-adopting states, play the most central role in policy diffusion networks." But this again raises an important question about the diffusion mechanism: Do states adopt similar policies because they learned from or emulated their peers, or are their policies similar simply because of shared national interest group pressure? This parallels "Galton's problem" of spurious correlation caused by common state characteristics (Braun and Gilardi 2006; Rose 1973). Scholars must sort out the independent effects of interest groups in state policy diffusion.

Scholars have developed interest group typologies to help understand their role in diffusion. For example, well-financed, multi-issue groups with a long time horizon, so-called "sustaining organizations," may be particularly effective in policy diffusion (Collingwood, El-Khatib, and O'Brien 2019). For example, the American Legislative Exchange Council develops influential model legislation from a conservative perspective on a variety of issues, including gun control, immigration, and labor law (Brown et al. 2019; Hertel-Fernandez 2019; Kroeger 2016).

Another important type of interest group for state policy diffusion is professional associations of state policymakers, such as the National Conference of State Legislatures, the National Association of State Budget Officers, and so forth ad infinitum. The national and highly specialized memberships of these associations position them well to develop cross-state political and policy information (Karch 2007b). These associations "provide state officials with opportunities – through meetings, publications, and other mechanisms – to learn about current developments in their policy area and the approaches that other states have taken to address particular problems" (Balla 2001: 223). These associations often promulgate "best practices," with at least implicit normative pressure to adopt "ideas in good currency" (Walker 1981: 76). Service in these associations gives policymakers "weak ties" to colleagues in other states, relationships that facilitate information flow (Granovetter 1973; Strang and Earl 1998). Even without explicit advocacy, these associations may exercise the "second face of power," setting the policy agenda through an imbalance of information (Bachrach and Barartz 1962). The result is that even bureaucrats working in state agencies have the "ability to shape [policymakers'] intellectual premises" because of their deep and long-standing understanding of the issues, their programs, and parallel programs in other states (Walker 1981: 78).

3.3.2 Policy Entrepreneurs

Interest groups are, at minimum, semi-permanent organizations with a constrained range of policy interests, but a related political player can also be a vector for policy information diffusion – the policy entrepreneur. Policy entrepreneurs are people who behave much like economic entrepreneurs, investing "resources – time, energy, reputation, and sometimes money – in the hope of future return" (Kingdon 1995: 122). But for policy entrepreneurs, this "return" is policy-related, not personal economic advantage. They are "energetic actors who engage in collaboration efforts in and around government to promote policy innovation" (Mintrom 2019: 307; see also Mintrom 2020). An entrepreneur's range of policy interests is much narrower than that of the typical interest group, and since they are individuals, they are less distracted by organizational maintenance and the other nonadvocacy activities that occupy many group leaders (Mohr 1969; Salisbury 1984). Entrepreneurs are particularly important in the early stages of policymaking, defining the problem and solution, setting the agenda, and building coalitions (Makse 2020; Mintrom 1997).

Policy entrepreneurs "are identifiable primarily by the actions they take, rather than by the positions they hold," and multiple entrepreneurs could be working on a policy, pursuing various interests (Mintrom and Vergari 1996: 423). An entrepreneur could be a legislator, a staffer, a bureaucrat, an interest group leader, or even just a private citizen with the resources and motivation to become active on an issue (Kingdon 1995). Makse (2020) finds that legislative policy "champions" (i.e., legislators acting as policy entrepreneurs) tend to be members of a relevant committee or have a professional background on the issue.

While few entrepreneurs will work on any given issue, they can have an outsized influence on policymaking (Freeman 1985; Mintrom 1997; Weissert 1991). As Walker (1981: 91) argues, "policy innovation in such a loosely coupled system usually requires, as a necessary condition, the intervention of a skillful political entrepreneur." In the chaotic world of state policymaking, issue-focused entrepreneurs can lead and influence the actions of others, with their drive and organization often being needed to overcome the policy status quo. In contrast to interest groups, which typically pursue incremental change in technical policy, entrepreneurs are especially interested in major policy change, including the adoption of new programs. For example, charter school reforms represented a significant policy change in the 1990s, and it was driven by entrepreneurial activity (Mintrom and Vergari 1996, 1998). In addition to diffusion theory, policy entrepreneurs play an important role in other major theories of policymaking, including advocacy coalition frameworks and punctuated equilibrium theory (Anderson, DeLeo, and Taylor 2020).

The state policy diffusion literature is replete with calls for more study of entrepreneurs (e.g., Karch 2007b; Mossberger 2000), but the idiosyncratic nature of entrepreneurialism makes this challenging. In the seminal state policy diffusion paper on the subject, Mintrom (1997) had to conduct a survey to identify policy entrepreneurs since no roster of them existed, as it does for other key actors in policymaking, such as lawmakers and bureaucrats. A precise operational definition of "policy entrepreneur" remains elusive, further retarding work in this area.

3.4 Policy Characteristics

One of the oldest controversies in the state policy diffusion literature involves the characteristics of the policies being diffused. Gray (1973a) began the discussion by criticizing Walker 1969's aggregation of eighty-eight policies into a single innovativeness measure, arguing that this loses informative variation among the diffusions. Graham, Shipan, and Volden (2012: 698) write that "the nature of the diffusion may depend fundamentally on the type of policy that is spreading," while Clark (1985: 63) claims that "the factors affecting diffusion appear to be highly variable from policy to policy area."

Variation across policy types raises both theoretical and methodological questions for the state policy diffusion literature. Theoretically, is there a set of common underlying processes for all policy diffusion (Eyestone 1977)? Or do some categories of policy have distinct processes, and if so, why? Methodologically, does policy heterogeneity mean that pooling policies for analysis yields biased results (Boehmke 2009a; Boehmke and Skinner 2012)? Can policy characteristics be controlled through regression analysis, and how can we model any hypothesized contingency effects (Bromley-Trujillo and Karch 2020)? These questions remain unanswered. Indeed, Makse and Volden (2011) argue that policy heterogeneity may explain some contradictory findings in the literature. Pacheco recommends studying "the conditional nature of policy diffusion dynamics by focusing on variations in *policy content*" (2017: 301, emphasis in the original). Paralleling Gray 1973a, some studies have examined multiple policy diffusions individually to "avoid the contextual nature of policy-specific studies" (Grossback, Nicholson-Crotty, and Peterson 2004: 528).

As noted previously, Rogers (2003: chapter 6) identifies five general innovation characteristics that can affect diffusion: relative advantage, compatibility with current practice, complexity, trialability, and observability (see also Makse and Volden 2011). State policy diffusion scholarship on these dimensions has been limited, presenting a great opportunity for future research. Scholars have studied the influence of other policy characteristics on state policy diffusion, including substantive policy categories (Boushey 2010; Callaghan, Karch, and Kroeger 2020; Mallinson 2016; Mooney and Lee 1995), policies on the same subject but with different ideological slants (Boushey and Luedtke 2011; Kreitzer 2015), distributive versus redistributive policy (Lieberman and Shaw 2000; Weyland 2005), judicial policy (Caldeira 1985; Canon and Baum 1981; Lutz 1997; Roch and Howard 2008), and policies that differ on visibility and facticity (Strebel and Widmer 2012), among other categorizations (Boushey 2016; Bromley-Trujillo and Karch 2020; Minkman, van Buuren, and Bekkers 2018). Furthermore, policy characteristics may change during the course of a lengthy diffusion, potentially affecting diffusion processes (Crain 1966; Bromley-Trujillo and Karch 2020). Future scholarship should develop more theoretically meaningful, consistent, and generalizable policy categories, perhaps focusing on Rogers' (2003) five characteristics. To date, the most sustained research on policy-contingent diffusion processes has focused on two characteristics – salience and complexity.

3.4.1 Issue Salience and Controversy

A policy debate is salient if voters are paying attention to it. Most state policy is made quietly, involving only limited groups of like-minded people (Rosenthal 2008). Even the informed public follows only, at most, a few issues in a legislative session, primarily through the media (Boushey 2010). How could a policy's salience affect its diffusion among the states? First, public opinion might be more relevant in debates over salient policy, since this would enhance policymakers' incentive to represent their constituents better (Pacheco 2013). Salience could also cause a diffusion to speed up if information travels across state lines more quickly for well-known policies (Boushey 2016; Mallinson 2016; Nicholson-Crotty 2009). On the other hand, salience might slow the diffusion of a disliked program. If so, analyses combining policies of different salience are biased toward finding no effect (Mallinson 2020b).

Closely related to a policy's salience is its level of controversy. Most simply, uncontroversial policies should diffuse more quickly because, by definition, they generate little opposition (Jacob 1988; Ka and Teske 2002). But controversy could also affect other dimensions of policy diffusion (Macinko and Silver 2015). For example, Hays (1996a, 1996b) finds less reinvention comprehensiveness for controversial issues than for noncontroversial ones. Controversy may influence whether policymakers respond to public or elite opinion (Mooney and Lee 2000). The extent of and mechanisms behind a diffusion may be contingent on controversy. For instance, several controversial morality issues (e.g., DOMA laws, medical marijuana legalization, and religious freedom restoration acts) diffused quickly in recent decades – but only up to a point (Hollander and Patapan 2016). Likewise, when a state adopts a controversial policy, its neighbors may become even *less* likely to do so, especially those neighbors with different ideology or partisanship (Fay 2018). Thus, controversial policies may sometimes diffuse quickly, but only among states that share an ideology. More research needs to be done to model these relationships appropriately.

3.4.2 Complexity

The technical complexity of a policy's debate may also affect its diffusion among the states. As Gormley (1986: 598) writes, "a highly complex policy issue is one that raises factual questions that cannot be answered by generalists." Since most elected policymakers are policy generalists, when technical information is crucial to making effective decisions, they are at a disadvantage. The meaning of policy "complexity" is uncertain and probably contextual, but it has been measured using item response theory (Plutzer et al. 2019), reading level scores (Hansen and Jansa 2019), and ad hoc data and argument (Mooney and Lee 2000).

Most scholarship on the diffusion of complex policy has focused on learning, with the central hypothesis being that complex policies diffuse more slowly because of difficult information needs (Boushey 2010; Makse and Volden 2011; Mallinson 2016; Shipan and Volden 2012). As Nicholson-Crotty (2009: 196) puts it, "simple policies naturally demand less policy learning because there is less to know." Hansen and Jansa (2019) find that complex policies are reinvented more often than are simpler ones, suggesting more learning is required with the former. For diffusion driven by competition or coercion, complexity may have other effects. As with controversy, complexity may affect the determinants of adoption (Taylor et al. 2012). For example, since expertise is helpful in understanding complex policy, greater staff capacity in the legislature and the agencies could have a salutary effect on adoption (Ka and Teske 2002). Interacting policy complexity and institutional capacity in a multi-policy analysis may provide a good test of this hypothesis (Arel-Bundock and Parinandi 2018). The interaction of complexity and salience may also influence the speed of a diffusion (Nicholson-Crotty 2009).

3.5 Methodology

Testing theories of state policy diffusion is challenging because of the complicated theoretical relationships involved and the empirical problems they cause. Furthermore, diverse methodological issues arise because this literature explores such a wide variety of research questions and phenomena. Gilardi (2016: 11) laments the haphazard use of mechanism indicators across studies: "the same indicators are used for different mechanisms, and different indicators are used for the same mechanism." Interstate dependencies are also modeled inconsistently. While most diffusion models include an independent variable that accounts for bordering or coregional states (Mooney 2001a; Sharkansky 1968), others identify the location of certain populations targeted by a policy (Berry and Baybeck 2005) or even use complex weight matrices to reflect hypothesized or empirical relationships (Desmarais, Harden, and Boehmke 2015; Drolc, Ganrud, and Williams 2020). More generally, decades apart, Gray (1994) and Graham, Shipan, and Volden (2013) argued that the field needs more qualitative and mixed-methods studies, such as Jacob 1988, Karch 2007a, and Karch and Rose 2019. In particular, quantitative studies seem unable to explain "true innovation," that is, the first state to adopt a new program (but see Parinandi 2020). Walker (1973: 1190) predicted that the range of theoretically interesting questions arising from state policy diffusion would make "some merging of ... techniques probably necessary to produce a full picture of this complicated diffusion process."

Policy diffusion is difficult to model using the standard correlational methods of political science because of the multiple types of interdependence that are of inherent theoretical interest (Rose 1973). An adoption decision may be related to decisions made by other actors, in both space (e.g., neighboring states) and time (e.g., earlier decisions by the federal government); standard models used in the field must assume away or model these interconnections precisely to estimate their parameters validly. For example, ordinary least squares regression will yield unbiased slope estimates only when all cases are independent of each other, something in direct contradiction of the diffusion hypothesis. Importantly, it is precisely these interdependencies in which state policy diffusion scholars have an interest (Pacheco 2017; Reich 2019). Whether a state's policy choices are influenced by the actions of its neighbors or the federal government matters to diffusion theory. The basic statistical problem is that while standard correlation analysis requires case independence, conditional on the model being correctly specified (Greene 2018: 26–27), interdependence is the theoretical expectation in much state policy diffusion research (Gleason and Howard 2014; Rose 1973).

The major methodological issues receiving sustained attention in this literature relate to using regression models to assess the various influences on state policy adoption. Modeling policy adoption properly with regression requires both including all causal factors involved and using the correct functional form. Getting either of these wrong can invalidate research conclusions (Berry 1994). For instance, Berry, Fording, and Hansen (2003) argue that model misspecification seriously misled early "race-to-the-bottom" scholars of policy competition. Furthermore, the slow computers, software/programming challenges, and general weakness in statistical training for political scientists of the era also hamstrung these early scholars.

Walker 1969 highlighted the first major challenge to modeling state policy adoption correctly: many factors affect adoption decisions besides other states' policies. The literature on the influences on state spending that originally inspired Walker 1969 identified various intrastate factors associated with policy choice (e.g., Dawson and Robinson 1963; Hofferbert 1966; Sharkansky 1968). Especially problematic is the argument that states learn from or emulate their neighbors because they share certain characteristics (Grossback, Nicholson-Crotty, and Peterson 2004). A test of the independent effect of learning or emulation must control for these common characteristics, otherwise any identified relationship could be spurious (Berry 1994; Braun and Gilardi 2006; Foster 1978). Volden, Ting, and Carpenter (2008) demonstrate this formally.

Another general methodological issue in the state policy diffusion literature relates to whether policies diffuse in unique patterns or through a set of common underlying process. In the first major controversy in the field, Gray (1973a) graphed several individual diffusions over time, demonstrating heterogeneity in their temporal adoption patterns. By pooling eighty-eight policies into a single innovativeness score, she argued that Walker lost crucial variation and nuance. There are two major concerns here: sample bias and heterogeneous processes

First, a sample of diffusions could be biased, that is, it might not be representative of all policy diffusions among the states. Recognizing this possibility, Walker 1969 (882) argued that his sample was selected with "no ideological bias" and with no determination about their "relative importance or desirability." In his comments on Gray's (1973a) critique, he further demonstrates an awareness of this problem (Walker 1973). But biases in diffusion selection likely exist. For example, Karch et al. 2016 claim that the entire field suffers from a "pro-innovation bias," only studying policies that are widely adopted (Rogers 2003: 106–18). Admirably, Boehmke et al. 2020 try to validate their sample of diffusions against the policy agendas of the US Congress and the Pennsylvania General Assembly. To date, no scholar has validly sampled from any sort of general population of state policy (Nicholson-Crotty 2009). Scholars have typically tried to address this concern, not by drawing probabilistic samples from a known population, but rather by simply analyzing larger samples of diffusions. Scholars have accumulated data on many diffusions over the decades, building from Walker 1969's original 88 policies all the way to the State Policy Innovation and Diffusion database (SPID), with 728 of them at last count (Boehmke et al. 2020). But of course, increasing sample size neither logically nor generally ensures representativeness, but with a finite population, as diffusions might be conceived to be, sample size is negatively correlated with bias. Furthermore, because policy diffusion data collection is laborious, scholars have often used the same data in multiple studies, whether on the lottery, renewable energy portfolio standards, or simply Walker's eighty-eight policies. The question of policy diffusion sample representativeness is fundamental to scholarship in this field.

The second statistical problem with pooling diffusions for analysis has to do with the potential for heterogeneous causal forces to be at work (Savage 1978). With the introduction of event history analysis to the field (Berry and Berry 1990), studies of single policy diffusions proliferated in the 1990s and 2000s. As a result, scholars began considering whether diffusion forces were constant, contingent, or just "an amalgam of causal effects" that varied across policy (Reich 2019: 21). Is there a single true process that all diffusions circle around stochastically, or are there multiple true effects for different types of policy or some other meaningful dimension? Pooling heterogeneous processes into a single analysis attenuates any estimated effect toward zero, decreasing statistical power. Thus, while the problem of policy sampling is strictly practical, the question of heterogeneous diffusion processes also has theoretical interest.

3.5.1 Modeling State Policy Adoption and Diffusion

Consider now the methodological evolution of policy adoption analysis, the largest and most persistent stream of scholarship on state policy diffusion, with special emphasis on modeling interstate dependency and causal mechanisms. This evolution has been motivated, not only by theoretical insights and empirical results, but also by periodic methodological innovation, primarily in how to model spatial and temporal dependency. These game-changing methodological innovations include, most obviously, Berry and Berry's (1990) introduction of event history analysis to the field, but also Volden's (2006) use of dyadic data and, potentially, the network analysis of Desmarais, Harden, and Boehmke (2015) and Boehmke et al. (2020). On the other hand, the literature has seen many methodological innovations that did not catch on, whether because they did not accomplish their goals or because they were too inconvenient for practical scholarly use (e.g., Foster 1978; Gray 1973a; Langer and Brace 2005; Light 1978; Mooney 2001a). LaCombe and Boehmke (2020) provide an extensive, detailed, and up-to-date review of the major diffusion models used in this literature in the past thirty years. Here, I place these models in the historical context of the state policy diffusion literature.

Walker 1969 uses factor analysis to identify regional clusters, culminating in an informal assessment of the interdependence of states' policy-making decisions. While his methodological approach might not pass muster today, it represented cutting-edge empirical analysis when published. Walker also tries to avoid spuriousness using partial correlations, but with only one control variable at a time. Multiple regression analysis was uncommon in published political science in 1969 due to computing hardware and software limitations. In the end, Walker's approach is purely correlational, with serious model underspecification.

Throughout the 1970s and 1980s, scholars tried to address the various methodological challenges of modeling policy adoption diffusion, using techniques ranging from time-series analysis (Gray 1973a, 1976) to cluster analysis (Light 1978) to cross-sectional regression and residual analysis (Foster 1978) to path models (Plotnick and Winters 1985). Other papers used various percentages, correlations, and partial correlations to draw conclusions as late as 1984 (e.g., Canon and Baum 1981; Clark and French 1984; Crain 1966; Dye 1966; Mohr 1969). These methodological fits and starts limited progress in, and failed to provide clear direction for, the field in this period, leading to several research dead ends.

In June 1990, the second most important article in the state policy diffusion literature was published in the *American Political Science Review* – Berry and Berry 1990. The epitome of theoretical and empirical clarity, Berry and Berry 1990 initiated the scholarly renaissance in the field that continues today. Theoretically, Berry and Berry use Mohr 1969's general theory of policy-making, which they apply to the diffusion of state lotteries. But their statistical innovation – the introduction of event history analysis (EHA) – is what has made Berry and Berry 1990 a bedrock of the field. As LaCombe and Boehmke (2020: 7) write, EHA has been "the workhorse method for studies of diffusion in political science." Berry and Berry 1990 introduced one type of EHA model, with a single, nonrepeating event as its dependent variable.[10]

EHA offered three major benefits for state policy diffusion research related to case-interdependence and model specification (Box-Steffensmeier and Jones 2004). First, EHA models time dependency using multiple time-series data. Second, it handles modeling rare events, like policy adoption, well. Third, and most crucially, it can include both internal state policy determinants (e.g., wealth or legislative professionalism) and external forces (e.g., federal incentives or neighboring states' policies) as independent variables. This was a major advance for the field. For the first time, a regression model of diffusion could be, if not fully specified, at least better specified. While perfect specification is a platonic ideal, EHA was a vast improvement for diffusion studies, even over cross-sectional multiple regression (Berry 1994).

The theoretical, statistical, and practical advantages of EHA over previous statistical approaches to modeling state policy diffusion led to the plethora of single-policy diffusion studies published in the 1990s and 2000s. Boehmke (2009a: 229) saw this as a problem, arguing that the literature has "reached a point of diminishing marginal returns from the standard EHA model." The main concern was whether the causal processes behind one diffusion were the same as those behind another, that is, the question of process heterogeneity.

To address this concern, Boehmke (2009a) introduces Pooled Event History Analysis (PEHA), where data from multiple policy diffusions are analyzed simultaneously. While the unit of analysis for Berry and Berry's single-policy EHA is the state/year, the unit of analysis for PEHA is the policy/state/year. Of

---

[10] See Box-Steffensmeier and Jones 2004 for a more general treatment of EHA models in political science.

course, this exacerbates dependency issues by adding correlation among cases on policy, but this can be incorporated using multi-level modeling (Gilardi 2010; Kreitzer and Boehmke 2016). PEHA has statistical advantages over EHA, including "parsimony and the ability to pool information and obtain precise estimates of the coefficients by increasing the number of observations" (Boehmke 2009a: 235). However, this approach generally requires the assumption of a common true coefficient value for each variable across policies, which heterogeneous processes could violate. PEHA averages coefficient estimates across policies, so with process heterogeneity, PEHA estimates will be biased toward the mean and inefficient (LaCombe and Boehmke 2020).

Thus, one fundamental problem with EHA and PEHA in this literature is that their results are biased by any heterogeneity among diffusion processes. Just as PEHA averages potentially diverse effects across policies, EHA and PEHA both average the influences of other states within any given designated group. For example, if spatial diffusion is operationalized with a "percentage of neighboring states having adopted" variable, its estimated coefficient will be the average influence of all of the neighboring states. So if Kentucky takes policy guidance from Tennessee but ignores its other six neighbors, the estimated coefficient for the "neighboring states" variable would be attenuated toward zero, as the positive Tennessee effect is averaged with the null effects of Kentucky's other neighbors. As a result, we might conclude that Kentucky does not learn from its neighbors at all, even though it does learn from Tennessee, a Type II error. Likewise, these biased estimates for each state are aggregated up to the national level in a PEHA or EHA, further averaging and attenuating the overall estimate of influence.

Volden 2006 introduced dyadic data to the study of state policy diffusion, although the approach had previously been used in international relations scholarship (Gilardi and Fuglister 2008).[11] Dyadic data highlight the directional relationship between two states. That is, whether State A learns from, emulates, or competes with State B is a distinct dyadic case from whether State B learns from, emulates, or competes with State A. Therefore, the unit of analysis is a *pair of states with a clear distinction between sender and receiver*. Thus, there are (N * [N–1]) cases (where N = number of states in the analysis), with, for example, the case Alabama-to-Alaska being distinct from Alaska-to-Alabama. This conception allows for the assessment of a state's influence on a peer's policymaking, but with the flexibility to assess relationships among any set of

---

[11] Studying judicial policy diffusion, Caldeira 1985 and Lutz 1987 foreshadow Volden 2006 by analyzing pairs of neighboring states and even using the term "dyad." However, they did not offer a reasonably general approach to modeling diffusion, nor did they serve as a building block for further policy diffusion research, as did Volden 2006.

sender states, such as regional or national leaders, laggards, neighbors, or something else. The dependent variable is a dummy indicating whether receiver-state policy moved closer to sender-state policy in a given time period. Thus, dyadic analysis is still EHA, but it uses a different unit of analysis to model the theoretical relationships among states more precisely.

By definition, dyadic data are not independent, and "failure to account for the dependence in the data dramatically underestimates the size of the standard errors and overstates the power of the test" (Erikson, Pinto, and Rader 2014: 457). Fixed effects in an EHA model may help with this (Tomz, Goldstein, and Rivers 2007). Analysts must also eliminate all dyadic cases where the sender state has not yet adopted the policy in question, since such a situation logically rules out learning, competing, or emulating (Boehmke 2009b). Likewise, Berry and Berry's (1990) EHA reduces bias and increases precision by dropping cases where the potential for adoption is zero (i.e., for state/years where the policy was already adopted).

Thus, dyadic data allow modeling how a state's decisions are influenced by the actions of another specific state, rather than averaging those effects across some group of sender states, like neighbors. The logical extension of this has yielded the newest approach to modeling state policy diffusion – network analysis (Desmarais, Harden, and Boehmke 2015). Network analysis assesses the sender-receiver relationship for all sets of states, not just pairs, allowing for testing of a range of hypotheses about diffusion pathways (LaCombe and Boehmke 2020). The unit of analysis is a policy diffusion (or as Desmarais, Harden, and Boehmke 2015 call it, a policy "cascade"), and the data are dyadic. The resulting estimated weight matrix representing the diffusion relationships among the states can be used in an EHA or PEHA model much as a "neighboring states" variable has been used, to test hypotheses about diffusion pathways. Not only does network analysis estimate these relationships precisely, but as LaCombe and Boehmke (2020: 16) point out, "different diffusion mechanisms imply different network connections," which can help test those hypotheses. For example, competition should be characterized by a reciprocal relationship among states, while learning could be unidirectional. Given its theoretical and empirical advantages, as well as the large number of policy diffusions now available to scholars (Boehmke et al. 2020), network analysis is ripe for creative use.

Geographic dependence is central to diffusion theory, but the statistical techniques commonly used in the state policy diffusion literature do not handle it particularly well, as noted. Spatial econometrics techniques have recently been used by some diffusion scholars to assess geographic dependence, offering "a potential middle ground between dyadic analysis of ties in the diffusion network and monadic analysis of the choices by individual units" (LaCombe and Boehmke 2020: 19). A spatial dependence weight matrix (deduced theoretically or estimated empirically via network analysis) is used to model the flow of policy, information, and influence (Arel-Bundock and Parinandi 2018; Pacheco 2017; Zhu et al. n.d.). Mitchell (2018) suggests using Moran's I to estimate whether any spatial correlation exists in a dataset before attempting to model it, although this would only reveal first-order relationships.

Some policy diffusions may be modeled best as a two-step process using some sort of Heckman model. For example, the first step might be passing a constitutional amendment permitting legislative action, and the second step would then be the passage of enabling legislation (Fay and Wenger 2016). These stages may be caused by different factors. Likewise, the unique influences on introductions and adoptions (Bromley-Trujillo and Karch 2020) and other processes (Pacheco 2012) could be modeled this way. The range of distinctive methodological challenges facing state policy diffusion scholars will likely continue to inspire methodological innovation to squeeze more information out of this sort of data.

4 Conclusion

This essay has organized and taken stock of the vast literature on state policy diffusion spawned by Walker 1969. The terrain has been complicated, with many subtly distinct questions, overlapping lines of inquiry, and fits and starts over time. This roadmap will help scholars better understand the field and the various relationships, contradictions, and contingencies found therein. Identifying surprising connections and new ideas in this literature will inspire and inform new scholarship. This essay also provides scholars with guidance about how to solidify the hard-won gains of this literature and use them to enrich our understanding of policymaking. While graduate students and junior scholars will benefit most from this essay, the scope of this literature is such that even senior scholars will learn something from it.

This essay comes at a propitious moment in the history of the field. Fifty years after Walker 1969, with a two-decade flurry of important new theory and method in the field, and a crop of top-notch young scholars working diligently on it, the time is ripe to throw down a marker as to where we have been and where we might go. I have seeded this essay with questions that demand future research, demonstrating both that the field is robust and that the insights of this literature inform a wide range of political science theory and practice. At root, this essay is a love letter to future state politics scholars. There is much productive, important work to do. Get busy!

Of course, this has not been a comprehensive examination of the state policy diffusion literature, much less the related literatures in comparative politics and international relations to which Walker 1969 also contributed. Given the goals and length of the essay, and the vastness of the literature, the best I could hope to accomplish was to review representative major works in the field, with an emphasis on the most up-to-date literature on each question.

On January 30, 1990, Jack Walker was killed in a car accident at the height of his career, largely unaware of what the full impact of his 1969 APSR article would be. His research interests had evolved from the study of diffusion to the related subject of interest group influence (Walker 1991). Walker died less than a year before the founding of the APSA's State Politics and Policy organized section and the publication of Berry and Berry 1990 and Rose 1991, critical events that were all natural extensions of Walker 1969. In his comment on Gray's (1973a) critique of his 1969 paper, Professor Walker expressed a modest delight: "It would be unduly coy of me not to express satisfaction at this evidence that another political scientist found my work stimulating enough to use it as a guide for further investigation" (Walker 1973: 1186). Had he the opportunity to see the widespread, progressive, and salutary impact that his article has had on political science, one hopes he would be pleased.

References

Allen, M. D., Pettus C., and Haider-Markel, D. (2004). Making the National Local: Specifying the Conditions for National Government Influence on State Policy. *State Politics and Policy Quarterly*, **4**(3), 318–44.

Allen, R., and Clark, J. (1981). State Policy Adoption and Innovation: Lobbying and Education. *State and Local Government Review*, **13**(1), 18–25.

Anderson, S. E., DeLeo, R. A., and Taylor, K. (2020). Policy Entrepreneurs, Legislators, and Agenda Setting: Information and Influence. *Policy Studies Journal*, **48**(3), 587–611.

Anzia, S. F., and Jackman, M.C. (2013). Legislative Organization and the Second Face of Power: Evidence from US State Legislatures. *Journal of Politics*, **75**(1), 210–24.

Arel-Bundock, V., and Parinandi, S. (2018). Conditional Tax Competition in the American States. *Journal of Public Policy*, **38**(2), 191–220.

Arsneault, S. (2001). Values and Virtues: The Politics of Abstinence-Only Sex Education. *American Review of Public Administration*, **31**(4), 436–54.

Atchison, A. L. (2017). Negating the Gender Citation Advantage in Political Science. *PS: Political Science and Politics*, **50**(2), 448–55.

Bachrach, P., and Baratz, M.S. (1962). The Two Faces of Power. *American Political Science Review*, **56**(4), 947–52.

Bailyn, B., and Allison, R. (2018). *The Essential Debate on the Constitution: Federalist and Anti-Federalist Speeches and Writing*, New York: Library of America.

Baker, G. E. (1966). *The Reapportionment Revolution Representation: Political Power, and the Supreme Court*, New York: Random House.

Balla, S. J. (2001). Interstate Professional Associations and the Diffusion of Policy Innovations. *American Politics Research*, **29**(3), 221–45.

Barrilleaux, C., and Rainey, C. (2014). The Politics of Need: Examining Governors' Decisions to Oppose 'Obamacare' Medicaid Expansion. *State Politics and Policy Quarterly*, **14**(4), 437–60.

Barwick, C., and Dawkins, R. (2020). Public Perceptions of State Court Impartiality and Court Legitimacy in an Era of Partisan Politics. *State Politics and Policy Quarterly*, **20**(1), 54–80.

Baumgartner, F. R. (2006). Commentaries: The *American Political Science Review* Citations Classics. *American Political Science Review*, **100**(4), 672.

Baumgartner, F. R., and Jones, B. D. (1993). *Agendas and Instability in American Politics*, Chicago: University of Chicago Press.

Baybeck, B., Berry, W. D., and Siegel, D.A. (2011). A Strategic Theory of Policy Diffusion via Intergovernmental Competition. *Journal of Politics*, **73**(1), 232–47.

Bennet, C. J. (1991). What is Policy Convergence and What Causes It? *British Journal of Political Science*, **21**(2), 215–33.

Berry, F. S. (1994). Sizing Up State Policy Innovation Research. *Policy Studies Journal*, **22**(3), 442–56.

Berry, F. S., and Berry, W. D. (1990). State Lottery Adoptions as Policy Innovations: An Event History Analysis. *American Political Science Review*, **84**(2), 395–415.

Berry, F. S., and Berry, W. D. (2007). Innovation and Diffusion Models in Policy Research. In P. A. Sabatier and C. M. Weible, eds., *Theories of the Policy Process*, 2nd ed., Boulder, CO: Westview, pp. 223–60.

Berry, F. S., and Berry, W. D. (2017). Innovation and Diffusion Models in Policy Research. In P. A. Sabatier and C. M. Weible, eds., *Theories of the Policy Process*, 4th ed., Boulder, CO: Westview, pp. 253–97.

Berry, W. D., and Baybeck, B. (2005). Using Geographic Information Systems to Study Interstate Competition. *American Political Science Review*, **99**(4), 505–19.

Berry, W. D., Fording, R. C., and Hansen, R. L. (2003). Reassessing the 'Race to the Bottom' in State Welfare Policy. *Journal of Politics*, **65**(2), 327–49.

Blau, P. M. (1977). *Heterogeneity and Inequality: Towards a Primitive Theory of Social Structure*, New York: Free Press.

Boehmke, F. J. (2009a). Approaches to Modeling the Adoption and Diffusion of Policies with Multiple Components. *State Politics and Policy Quarterly*, **9**(2), 229–52.

Boehmke, F. J. (2009b). Policy Emulation or Policy Convergence? Potential Ambiguities in the Dyadic Event History Approach to State Policy Emulation. *Journal of Politics*, **71**(3), 1125–40.

Boehmke, F. J., Brockway, M., Desmarais, B. A., et al. (2020). SPID: A New Database for Inferring Public Policy Innovativeness and Diffusion Networks. *Policy Studies Journal*, **48**(2), 517–45.

Boehmke, F. J., and Pacheco, J. (2016). *Policy Diffusion and Crafted Talk*, Typescript. Department of Political Science, University of Iowa.

Boehmke, F. J., and Skinner, P. (2012). State Policy Innovativeness Revisited. *State Politics and Policy Quarterly*, **12**(3), 303–29.

Boehmke, F. J., and Witmer, R. (2004). Disentangling Diffusion: The Effects of Social Learning and Economic Competition on State Policy Innovation and Expansion. *Political Research Quarterly*, **57**(1), 39–51.

Bouche, V., and Volden, C. (2011). Privatization and the Diffusion of Innovations. *Journal of Politics*, **73**(2), 428–42.

Bourdeaux, C., and Chikoto, G. (2008). Legislative Influences on Performance Management Reform. *Public Administration Review*, **68**(2), 253–65.

Boushey, G. (2010). *Policy Diffusion Dynamics in America*, New York: Cambridge University Press.

Boushey, G. (2012). Punctuated Equilibrium Theory and the Diffusion of Innovations. *Policy Studies Journal*, **40**(1), 127–46.

Boushey, G. (2016). Targeted for Diffusion? How the Use and Acceptance of Stereotypes Shape the Diffusion of Criminal Justice Policy Innovations in the American States. *American Political Science Review*, **110**(1), 198–214.

Boushey, G., and Luedtke, A. (2011). Immigrants across the U.S. Federal Laboratory: Explaining State-Level Innovation in Immigration Policy. *State Politics and Policy Quarterly*, **11**(4), 390–414.

Box-Steffensmeier, J. M., and Jones, B. S. (2004). *Event History Modeling: A Guide for Social Scientists*, New York: Cambridge University Press.

Braman, E., and Nelson, T.E. (2007). Mechanisms of Motivated Reasoning? Analogical Perception in Discrimination Disputes. *American Journal of Political Science*, **51**(4), 940–56.

Braun, D., and Gilardi, F. (2006). Taking "Galton's Problem" Seriously: Towards a Theory of Policy Diffusion. *Journal of Theoretical Politics*, **18**(3), 298–322.

Bricker, C., and LaCombe, S. (2020). The Ties that Bind Us: The Influence of Perceived State Similarity on Policy Diffusion. *Political Research Quarterly*, Forthcoming.

Bromley-Trujillo, R., and Karch, A. (2020). Salience, Scientific Uncertainty, and the Agenda-Setting Power of Science. *Policy Studies Journal*, Forthcoming.

Brown, C. R., Stoutenborough, J. W., Bromley-Trujillo, R., and Kirkpatrick, K. J. (2019). *The Use of Model Legislation to Draft Policy Beneficial to Corporate Interests: Rethinking the Influence of Special Interest Groups through a Study of the American Legislative Exchange Council (ALEC)*, presented at the Annual Meetings of the Midwest Political Science Association (Chicago, IL).

Bulman-Posen, J. (2014). Partisan Federalism. *Harvard Law Review*, **127**(4), 1077–146.

Burstein, P. (2020). The Determinants of Public Policy: What Matters and How Much. *Policy Studies Journal*, **48**(10), 87–110.

Burt, R. S. (1987). Social Contagion and Innovation: Cohesion versus Structural Equivalence. *American Journal of Sociology*, **92**(6), 1287–335.

Butler, D. M., Volden, C., Dynes, A. M., and Shor, B. (2017). Ideology, Learning, and Policy Diffusion: Experimental Evidence. *American Journal of Political Science*, **61**(1), 37–49.

Butler, D. M., and Pereira, M.M. (2018). TRENDS: How Does Partisanship Influence Policy Diffusion? *Political Research Quarterly*, **71**(4), 801–12.

Caldeira, G. A. (1985). The Transmission of Legal Precedent: A Study of State Supreme Courts. *American Political Science Review*, **79**(1), 178–93.

Callaghan, T., Karch, A., and Kroeger, M. 2020. Model State Legislation and Interstate Tensions over the Affordable Care Act, Common Core, and the Second Amendment. *Publius*, **50**(3), 518–39.

Canon, B. C., and Baum, L. (1981). Patterns of Adoption of Tort Law Innovations: An Application of Diffusion Theory to Judicial Doctrines. *American Political Science Review*, **75**(4), 975–87.

Carley, S., Nicholson-Crotty, S., and Miller, C.J. (2017). Adoption, Reinvention and Amendment of Renewable Portfolio Standards in the American States. *Journal of Public Policy*, **37**(4), 431–58.

Carson, J. L., and Kleinerman, B. A. (2002). A Switch in Time Saves Nine: Institutions, Strategic Actors, and FDR's Court-Packing Plan. *Public Choice*, **113**(2), 301–24.

Chiuri, M. C., Ferri, G., and Majnoni, G. (2001). *The Macroeconomic Impact of Bank Capital Requirements in Emerging Economies*, World Bank, Policy Research Working Paper 2605.

Clark, J. (1985). Policy Diffusion and Program Scope: Research Directions. *Publius*, **15**(3), 61–70.

Clark, J., and French, J. L. (1984). Innovation and Program Content in State Tax Policies. *State and Local Government Review*, **16**(1), 11–16.

Coates, M., and Pearson-Merkowitz, S. (2017). Policy Spillover and Gun Migration: The Interstate Dynamics of State Gun Control Policies. *Social Science Quarterly*, **98**(2), 500–12.

Collingwood, L., El-Khatib, S. O., and Gonzalez O'Brien, B. (2019). Sustained Organizational Influence: American Legislative Exchange Council and the Diffusion of Anti-Sanctuary Policy. *Policy Studies Journal*, **47**(3), 735–73.

Crabtree, C., and Nelson, M. J. (2019). Judging Judicial Review in the American States. *State Politics and Policy Quarterly*, **19**(3), 287–311.

Crain, R. L. (1966). Fluoridation: The Diffusion of an Innovation among Cities. *Social Forces*, **44**(4), 467–76.

Dahl, R. A. (1961). *Who Governs?* New Haven, CT: Yale University Press.

Davis, A. J. (1930). The Evolution of the Institution of Mothers' Pensions in the United States. *American Journal of Sociology*, **35**(4), 573–82.

Dawson, R. E., and Robinson, J. A. (1963). Interparty Competition, Economic Variables, and Welfare Policy in the American States. *Journal of Politics*, **25**(2), 265–89.

Desmarais, B. A., Harden, J. J., and Boehmke, F. J. (2015). Persistent Policy Pathways: Inferring Diffusion Networks in the American States. *American Political Science Review*, **109**(2), 392–406.

DiMaggio, P. J., and Powell, W. W. (1983). The Iron Cage Revisited: Institutional Isomorphism and Collective Rationality in Organizational Fields. *American Sociological Review*, **48**(2), 147–60.

Dolowitz, D., and Marsh, D. (1996). Who Learns What from Whom: A Review of the Policy Transfer Literature. *Political Studies*, **44**(2), 343–57.

Drolc, C. A., Gandrud, C., and Williams, L. K. (2020). Taking Time (and Space) Seriously: How Scholars Falsely Infer Policy Diffusion from Model Misspecification. *Policy Studies Journal*, Forthcoming.

Dunlop, C. A., and Radaelli, C. M. (2017). Learning in the Bath-Tub: The Micro and Macro Dimensions of the Causal Relationships between Learning and Policy Change. *Policy and Society*, **36**(2), 304–19.

Dye, T. R. (1966). *Politics, Economics, and the Public: Policy Outcomes in the American States*. Chicago: Rand McNally & Co.

Dye, T. R. (1979). Politics vs. Economics: The Development of the Literature on Policy Determinism. *Policy Studies Journal*, **7**(4), 652–62.

Dye, T. R. (1984). Party and Policy in the States. *Journal of Politics*, **46**(4), 1097–116.

Dye, T. R. (1990). *American Federalism: Competition among Governments*. Lexington, MA: Lexington Books.

Elazar, D. J. (1984). *American Federalism: A View from the States*, 3rd ed., New York: Harper & Row.

Ellison, J. M., and Spohn, R. E. (2017). Borders Up in Smoke: Marijuana Enforcement in Nebraska after Colorado's Legalization of Medicinal Marijuana. *Criminal Justice Policy Review*, **28**(9), 847–65.

Engel, K. H. (1997). State Environmental Standard-Setting: Is There a 'Race' and Is It to the 'Bottom?' *Hastings Law Journal*, **48**(2), 271–398.

Erikson, R. S., Pinto, P. M., and Rader, K. T. (2014). Dyadic Analysis in International Relations: A Cautionary Tale. *Political Analysis*, **22**(4), 457–63.

Erikson, R. S., Wright, G. C., and McIver, J. P. (1993). *Statehouse Democracy: Public Opinion in the American States*. New York: Cambridge University Press.

Eyestone, R. (1977). Confusion, Diffusion, and Innovation. *American Political Science Review*, **71**(2), 441–47.

Fabricant, S. (1952). *The Trend in Government Activity in the United States since 1900*. New York: National Bureau of Economic Research.

Fay, D. L. (2018). Moves and Countermoves: Countermovement Diffusion of State Constitutional Amendments. *Policy Studies Journal*, **46**(2), 354–77.

Fay, D. L., and Wenger, J. B. (2016). The Political Structure of Policy Diffusion. *Policy Studies Journal*, **44**(3), 349–65.

Fenton, J. (1966). *Midwest Politics*. New York: Holt, Rinehart, and Winston.

Fenton, J. H., and Chamberlayne, D.W. (1969). The Literature Dealing with the Relationships between Political Processes and Socioeconomic Conditions & Public Policies in the American States: A Bibliographic Essay. *Polity*, **1**(3), 388–404.

Filindra, A. (2013). Immigration Social Policy in the American States: Race Politics and State TANF and Medicaid Eligibility Rules for Legal Permanent Residents. *State Politics and Policy Quarterly*, **13**(1), 26–48.

Finnemore, M., and Sikkink, K. (1998). International Norm Dynamics and Political Change. *International Organizations*, **52**(4), 887–917.

Fisher, B. S., and Sloan, III, J. J. (2018). *Arming the Ivory Tower: Theoretical and Empirical Analyses of State-Level Pro-Firearms-on-Campus Legislative Activity*, Presented at the annual meetings of the American Society of Criminology (Atlanta, GA).

Foster, J. L. (1978). Regionalism and Innovation in the American States. *Journal of Politics*, **40**(1), 179–87.

Franzese, Jr., R. J., and Hays, J. C. (2006). Strategic Interactions among EU Governments in Active Labor Market Policymaking: Subsidiarity and Policy Coordination under the European Employment Strategy. *European Union Politics*, **7**(2), 167–89.

Freeman, P. K. (1985). Interstate Communication among State Legislators Regarding Energy Policy Innovation. *Publius*, **15**(4), 99–111.

Fry, B. R., and Winters, R. F. (1970). The Politics of Redistribution. *American Political Science Review*, **64**(2), 508–22.

Garrett, K. N., and Jansa, J. M. (2015). Interest Group Influence in Policy Diffusion Networks. *State Politics and Policy Quarterly*, **15**(3), 387–417.

Ghasemi, A., and Zahediasl, S. (2012). Normality Tests for Statistical Analysis: A Guide for Non-Statisticians. *International Journal of Endocrinology and Metabolism*, **10**(2), 486–89.

Gilardi, F. (2010). Who Learns What in Policy Diffusion Processes? *American Journal of Political Science*, **54**(3), 650–66.

Gilardi, F. (2016). Four Ways We Can Improve Policy Diffusion Research. *State Politics and Policy Quarterly*, **16**(1), 8–21.

Gilardi, F., and Fuglister, K. (2008). Empirical Modeling of Policy Diffusion in Federal States: The Dyadic Approach. *Swiss Political Science Review*, **14**(3), 413–50.

Gilardi, F., Shipan, C. R., and Wueest, B. (2020). Policy Diffusion: The Issue-Definition Stage. *American Journal of Political Science*, Forthcoming.

Gilardi, F., and Wasserfallen, F. (2019). The Politics of Diffusion. *European Journal of Political Research*, **58**(4), 1245–56.

Gillette, C. P. (1991). In Partial Praise of Dillon's Rule, or, Can Public Choice Theory Justify Government? *Chicago-Kent Law Review*, **57**(3), 959–1010.

Gleason, S. A., and Howard, R.M. (2014). State Supreme Courts and Shared Networking: The Diffusion of Education Policy. *Albany Law Review*, **78**(4), 1485–512.

Glick, D. M., and Friedland, Z. (2014). How Often Do States Study Each Other? Evidence of Policy Knowledge Diffusion. *American Politics Research*, **42** (6), 956–85.

Glick, H. R., and Hays, S. P. (1991). Innovation and Reinvention in State Policymaking: Theory and the Evolution of Living Will Laws. *Journal of Politics*, **53**(3), 835–50.

Goggin, M. L., Bowman, A. O., Lester, J., and O'Toole, L. (1990). *Implementation Theory and Practice: Toward a Third Generation*. Glenview, IL: Scott Foresman and Co.

Gormley, Jr., W. T. (1986). Regulatory Issue Networks in a Federal System. *Polity*, **18**(4), 595–620.

Graham, E. R., Shipan, C. R., and Volden, C. (2013). The Diffusion of Policy Diffusion Research in Political Science. *British Journal of Political Science*, **43**(3), 673–701.

Granovetter, M. S. (1973). The Strength of Weak Ties. *American Journal of Sociology*, **78**(6), 1360–80.

Gray, V. (1973a). Innovation in the States: A Diffusion Study. *American Political Science Review*, **67**(4), 1174–85.

Gray, V. (1973b). Rejoinder to 'Comment' by Jack L. Walker. *American Political Science Review*, **67**(4), 1192–93.

Gray, V. (1974). Expenditures and Innovation as Dimensions of 'Progressivism': A Note on the American States. *American Journal of Political Science*, **18**(4), 693–99.

Gray, V. (1976). Models of Comparative State Politics: A Comparison of Cross-Sectional and Time Series Analyses. *American Journal of Political Science*, **20**(2), 235–56.

Gray, V. (1994). Competition, Emulation, and Policy Innovation. In L. C. Dodd and C. Jillison, eds., *New Perspectives on American Politics*. Washington, DC: CQ Press, pp. 230–48.

Greene, W. H. (2018). *Econometric Analysis*. 8th ed., New York: Pearson.

Grodzins, M. (1966.) *The American System*. Chicago: Rand-McNally.

Grossback, L. J., Nicholson-Crotty, S., and Peterson, D.A.M. (2004). Ideology and Learning in Policy Diffusion. *American Politics Research*, **32**(5), 521–45.

Grupp, F. W., and Richards, A. R. (1975). Variations in Elite Perceptions of American States as Referents for Public Policy Making. *American Political Science Review*, **69**(3), 850–58.

Hannah, A. L., and Mallinson, D. J. (2018). Defiant Innovation: The Adoption of Medical Marijuana Laws in the American States. *Policy Studies Journal*, **46**(2), 402–23.

Hansen, E. R., and Jansa, J. M. (2019). *Bill Complexity and Text Borrowing in State Policy Diffusion*. Presented at the annual meetings of the Midwest Political Science Association (Chicago).

Hays, S. P. (1996a). Influences on Reinvention during the Diffusion of State Policy Innovations. *Political Research Quarterly*, **49**(3), 613–32.

Hays, S. P. (1996b). Patterns of Reinvention: The Nature of Evolution during Policy Diffusion. *Policy Studies Journal*, **24**(4), 551–66.

Hays, S. P., and Glick, H. R. (1997). The Role of Agenda Setting in Policy Innovation: An Event History Analysis of Living-Will Laws. *American Politics Quarterly*, **25**(4), 497–516.

Heikkila, T., and Gerlak, A. K. (2013). Building a Conceptual Approach to Collective Learning: Lessons for Public Policy Scholars. *Policy Studies Journal*, **41**(3), 484–512.

Hertel-Fernandez, A. (2019). *State Capture: How Conservative Activists, Big Businesses and Wealthy Donors Reshaped the American States – and the Nation*. New York: Oxford University Press.

Hinkle, R. K. (2015). Into the Words: Using Statutory Text to Explore the Impact of Federal Courts on State Policy Diffusion. *American Journal of Political Science*, **59**(4), 1002–21.

Hinkle, R. K., and Nelson, M. J. (n.d.). The Relational Foundations of Policy Impact. University at Buffalo, SUNY, Department of Political Science. Typescript.

Hofferbert, R. I. (1966). The Relation between Public Policy and Some Structural and Environmental Variables in the American States. *American Political Science Review*, **60**(1), 73–82.

Hollander, R., and Patapan, H. (2016). Morality Policy and Federalism: Innovation, Diffusion, and Limits. *Publius*, **47**(1), 1–26.

Iyengar, S. (1990). The Accessibility Bias in Politics: Television News and Public Opinion. *International Journal of Public Opinion Research*, 2(1), 1–15.

Jacob, H. (1988). *Silent Revolution: The Transformation of Divorce Law in the United States*. Chicago: University of Chicago Press.

Jansa, J. M., Hansen, E. R., and Gray, V. H. (2019). Copy and Paste Lawmaking: Legislative Professionalism and Policy Reinvention in the States. *American Politics Research*, **47**(4), 739–67.

Jensen, J. M. (2016). *The Governors' Lobbyists: Federal-State Relations Offices and Governors Associations in Washington*. Ann Arbor: University of Michigan Press.

Ka, S., and Teske, P. (2002). Ideology and Professionalism: Electricity Regulation and Deregulation over Time in the American States. *American Politics Research*, **30**(3), 323–43.

Kahneman, D. (2011). *Thinking Fast and Slow*. New York: Farrar, Straus, and Giroux.

Karch, A. 2006. National Intervention and the Diffusion of Policy Innovations. *American Politics Research*, **34**(4), 403–26.

Karch, A. (2007a). *Democratic Laboratories: Policy Diffusion among the American States*. Ann Arbor: University of Michigan Press.

Karch, A. (2007b). Emerging Issues and Future Directions in State Policy Diffusion Research. *State Politics and Policy Quarterly*, **7**(1), 54–80.

Karch, A. (2012). Vertical Diffusion and the Policy-Making Process: The Politics of Embryonic Stem Cell Research. *Political Research Quarterly*, **65**(1), 48–61.

Karch, A., and Cravens, M. (2014). Rapid Diffusion and Policy Reform: The Adoption and Modification of Three Strikes Laws. *State Politics and Policy Quarterly*, **14**(4), 461–91.

Karch, A., Nicholson-Crotty, S. C., Woods, N. D., and Bowman, A. O. (2016). Policy Diffusion and the Pro-Innovation Bias. *Political Research Quarterly*, **69**(1), 83–95.

Karch, A., and Rose, S. (2019.) *Responsive States: Federalism and Public Policy*. New York: Cambridge University Press.

Karch, A., and Rosenthal, A. (2016). Vertical Diffusion and the Shifting Politics of Electronic Commerce. *State Politics and Policy Quarterly*, **16**(1), 22–43.

Katz, E., Levin, M. L., and Hamilton, H. (1963). Traditions of Research on the Diffusion of Innovation. *American Sociological Review*, **28**(2), 237–52.

Key, Jr., V. O. (1949). *Southern Politics*. New York: Knopf.

Kim, H. J., and Grofman, B. (2019). The Political Science 400: With Citation Counts by Cohort, Gender, and Sub-Field. *PS: Political Science and Politics*, **52**(2), 296–311.

Kim, J., McDonald, III, B. D., and Lee, J. (2018). The Nexus of State and Local Capacity in Vertical Policy Diffusion. *American Review of Public Administration*, **48**(2), 188–200.

Kincaid, J. (2017). The Eclipse of Dual Federalism by One-Way Cooperative Federalism. *Arizona State Law Journal*, **49**(3), 1061.

Kingdon, J. W. (1995). *Agendas, Alternatives, and Public Policies*, 2nd ed., New York: HarperCollins.

Krehbiel, K. (1991). *Information and Legislative Organization*. Ann Arbor: University of Michigan Press.

Kreitzer, R. J. (2015). Politics and Morality in State Abortion Policy. *State Politics and Policy Quarterly*, **15**(1), 41–66.

Kreitzer, R. J., and Boehmke, F.J. (2016). Modeling Heterogeneity in Pooled Event History Analysis. *State Politics and Policy Quarterly*, **16**(1), 121–41.

Kroeger, M. A. (2016). Plagiarizing Policy: Model Legislation in State Legislatures. Department of Politics, Princeton University. Typescript.

Kuhn, T. S. (1970). *The Structure of Scientific Revolutions*, 2nd ed., Chicago: University of Chicago Press.

Kurtz, K. T., Cain, B. E., and Neimi, R. G., eds. (2007). *Institutional Change in American Politics: The Case of Term Limits*. Ann Arbor: University of Michigan Press.

LaCombe, S., and Boehmke, F. J. (2020). Learning and Diffusion Models. In L. Curini and R. Franzese, eds., *Sage Handbook of Research Methods for Political Science and International Relations*. New York: Sage, chapter 20.

Langer, L., and Brace, P. (2005). The Preemptive Power of State Supreme Courts: Adoption of Abortion and Death Penalty Legislation. *Policy Studies Journal*, **33**(3), 317–40.

Leiser, S. (2017). The Diffusion of State Tax Incentives for Business. *Public Finance Review*, **45**(3), 334–63.

Levi-Faur, D. (2015). Jack Walker, "The Diffusion of Innovations among the American States." In M. Lodge, E. C. Page, and S. J. Balla, eds., *The Oxford Handbook of Classics in Public Policy and Administration*. New York: Oxford University Press, pp. 235–55.

Lieberman, R. C., and Shaw, G.M. (2000). Looking Inward, Looking Outward: The Politics of Welfare Innovation under Devolution. *Political Research Quarterly*, **53**(2), 215–40.

Light, A. R. (1978). Intergovernmental Sources of Innovation in State Administration. *American Politics Quarterly*, **6**(2), 147–66.

Lindblom, C. E. (1959). The Science of Muddling Through. *Public Administration Review*, **19**(2), 79–88.

Linder, F., Desmarais, B., Burgess, M., and Giraudy, E. (2020). Text as Policy: Measuring Policy Similarity through Bill Text Reuse. *Policy Studies Journal*, **48**(2), 546–74.

Lockard, D. (1959). *New England State Politics*. Princeton, NJ: Princeton University Press.

Lowery, D., Gray, V., and Baumgartner, F. R. (2010). Policy Attention in State and Nation: Is Anyone Listening to the Laboratories of Democracy? *Publius*, **41**(2), 286–310.

Lowi, T. J. (1969). *The End of Liberalism*. New York: Norton.

Lutz, J. L. (1986). The Spatial and Temporal Diffusion of Selected Licensing Laws in the United States. *Political Geography Quarterly*, **5**(2), 141–59.

Lutz, J. L. (1987). Regional Leadership Patterns in the Diffusion of Public Policies. *American Politics Quarterly*, **15**(3), 387–98.

Lutz, J. L. (1997). Regional Leaders in the Diffusion of Tort Innovations among the United States. *Publius*, **27**(1), 39–58.

Macinko, J., and Silver, D. (2015). Diffusion of Impaired Driving Laws among US States. *American Journal of Public Health*, **105**(9), 1893–900.

Maggetti, M., and Gilardi, F. (2016). Problems (and Solutions) in the Measurement of Policy Diffusion Mechanisms. *Journal of Public Policy*, **36**(1), 87–107.

Makse, T. (2020). Expertise and the Championing of Innovations in State Legislatures. *Policy Studies Journal*, Forthcoming.

Makse, T., and Volden, C. (2011). The Role of Policy Attributes in the Diffusion of Innovations. *Journal of Politics*, **73**(1), 108–24.

Mallinson, D. J. (2016). Building a Better Speed Trap: Measuring Policy Adoption Speed in the American States. *State Politics and Policy Quarterly*, **16**(1), 98–120.

Mallinson, D. J. (2020a). Policy Innovation Adoption across the Diffusion Life Course. *Policy Studies Journal*, Forthcoming.

Mallinson, D. J. (2020b). Who Are Your Neighbors? The Role of Ideology and Decline of Geographic Proximity in the Diffusion of Policy Innovations. *Policy Studies Journal*, Forthcoming.

Mayhew, D. R. (1974). *Congress: The Electoral Connection*. New Haven, CT: Yale University Press.

McCann, P. J. C., Shipan, C. H., and Volden, C. (2015). Top-Down Federalism: State Policy Responses to National Government Discussions. *Publius*, **45**(4), 495–525.

McVoy, E. C. (1940). Patterns of Diffusion in the United States. *American Sociological Review*, **5**(2), 219–27.

Meseguer, C. (2006). Rational Learning and Bounded Learning in the Diffusion of Policy Innovations. *Rationality and Society*, **18**(1), 35–66.

Michener, J. (2018). *Fragmented Democracy: Medicaid, Federalism, and Unequal Politics*. New York: Cambridge University Press.

Miller, S. M., Nicholson-Crotty, J., and Nicholson-Crotty, S. (2018). The Consequences of Legislative Term Limits for Policy Diffusion. *Political Research Quarterly*, **71**(3), 573–85.

Minkman, E., van Buuren, M. W., and Bekkers, V. J. J. M. (2018). Policy Transfer Routes: An Evidence-Based Conceptual Model to Explain Policy Adoption. *Policy Studies*, **39**(2), 222–50.

Mintrom, M. (1997). Policy Entrepreneurs and Policy Diffusion. *American Journal of Political Science*, **41**(3), 738–70.

Mintrom, M. (2019). So You Want to Be a Policy Entrepreneur? *Policy Design and Practice*, **2**(4), 307–23.

Mintrom, M. (2020). *Policy Entrepreneurs and Dynamic Change*. New York: Cambridge University Press.

Mintrom, M., and Vergari, S. (1996). Advocacy Coalitions, Policy Entrepreneurs, and Policy Change. *Policy Studies Journal*, **24**(3), 420–34.

Mintrom, M., and Vergari, S. (1998). Policy Networks and Innovation Diffusion: The Case of State Education Reforms. *Journal of Politics*, **60**(1), 126–48.

Mitchell, J. L. (2018). Does Policy Diffusion Need Space? Spatializing the Dynamics of Policy Diffusion. *Policy Studies Journal*, **46**(2), 424–50.

Mohr, L. B. (1969). Determinants of Innovation in Organizations. *American Political Science Review*, **63**(1), 111–26.

Monogan, J. E., Konisky, D.M., and Woods, N.D. (2017). Gone with the Wind: Federalism and the Strategic Location of Air Polluters. *American Journal of Political Science*, **61**(2), 257–270.

Mooney, C. Z. (1991). Information Sources in State Legislative Decision-making. *Legislative Studies Quarterly*, **16**(3), 445–55.

Mooney, C. Z. (2001a). Modeling Regional Effects on State Policy Diffusion. *Political Research Quarterly*, **54**(1), 103–24.

Mooney, C. Z. (2001b). *State Politics and Policy Quarterly* and the Study of State Politics: The Editor's Introduction. *State Politics and Policy Quarterly*, **1**(1), 1–4.

Mooney, C. Z. (2009). Term Limits as a Boon to Legislative Scholarship: A Review. *State Politics and Policy Quarterly*, **9**(2), 204–28.

Mooney, C. Z., and Lee, M. (1995). Legislating Morality in the American States: The Case of Pre-*Roe* Abortion Regulation Reform. *American Journal of Political Science*, **39**(3), 599–627.

Mooney, C. Z., and Lee, M. (1999). Morality Policy Reinvention: State Death Penalties. *Annals of the American Academy of Political and Social Science*, **566**, 80–92.

Mooney, C. Z., and Lee, M. (2000). The Influence of Values on Consensus and Contentious Morality Policy: U.S. Death Penalty Reform, 1956–82. *Journal of Politics*, **62**(1), 223–39.

Mossberger, K. (1999). State-Federal Diffusion and Policy Learning: From Enterprise Zones to Empowerment Zones. *Publius*, **29**(3), 31–50.

Mossberger, K. (2000). *The Politics of Ideas and the Spread of Enterprise Zones*. Washington, DC: Georgetown University Press.

New State Ice Co. v. Liebmann, 285 U.S. 262 (1932).

Nicholson-Crotty, S. (2009). The Politics of Diffusion: Public Policy in the American States. *Journal of Politics*, **71**(1), 192–205.

Nicholson-Crotty, S. (2012). Leaving Money on the Table: Learning from Recent Refusals of Federal Grants in the American States. *Publius*, **42**(3), 449–66.

Nicholson-Crotty, S. C., and Carley, S. (2016). Effectiveness, Implementation, and Policy Diffusion: Or 'Can We Make That Work for Us?' *State Politics and Policy Quarterly*, **16**(1), 78–97.

Nicholson-Crotty, S. C., Woods, N. D., Bowman A. O., and Karch, A. (2014). Policy Innovativeness and Interstate Compacts. *Policy Studies Journal*, **42**(2), 305–24.

Nisbett, R. E., and Ross, L. (1980). *Human Inference: Strategies and Shortcomings of Social Judgment*. Engelwood Cliffs, NJ: Prentice-Hall.

Niskanen, Jr., W. A. (1971). *Bureaucracy and Representative Government*. New Brunswick, NJ: Aldine/Transaction.

Nownes, A. J. (2012). *Interest Groups in American Politics: Pressure and Power*, 2nd ed., New York: Routledge.

Pacheco, J. (2011). Using National Surveys to Measure Dynamic U.S. State Public Opinion: A Guideline for Scholars and an Application. *State Politics and Policy Quarterly*, **11**(4), 415–39.

Pacheco, J. (2012). The Social Contagion Model: Exploring the Role of Public Opinion on the Diffusion of Antismoking Legislation across the American States. *Journal of Politics*, **74**(1), 187–202.

Pacheco, J. (2013). The Thermostatic Model of Responsiveness in the American States. *State Politics and Policy Quarterly*, **13**(3), 306–32.

Pacheco, J. (2017). Free-Riders or Competitive Races? Strategic Interaction across the American States on Tobacco Policy Making. *State Politics and Policy Quarterly*, **17**(3), 299–318.

Parinandi, S. C. (2013). Conditional Bureaucratic Discretion and State Welfare Diffusion under AFDC. *State Politics and Policy Quarterly*, **13**(2), 244–61.

Parinandi, S. C. (2020). Policy Inventing and Borrowing among State Legislatures. *American Journal of Political Science*, Forthcoming.

Patton, D. (2007). The Supreme Court and Morality Policy Adoption in the American States: The Constitutional Context. *Political Research Quarterly*, **60**(3), 468–88.

Peterson, P. E. (1981). *City Limits*. Chicago: University of Chicago Press.

Peterson, P. E., and Rom, M. C. (1989). American Federalism, Welfare Policy, and Residential Choices. *American Political Science Review*, **83**(3), 711–28.

Pierotti, R. S. (2013). Increasing Rejection of Intimate Partner Violence: Evidence of Cultural Diffusion. *American Sociological Review*, **78**(2), 240–65.

Plotnick, R. D., and Winters, R. F. (1985). A Politico-Economic Theory of Income Redistribution. *American Political Science Review*, **79**(2), 458–73.

Plutzer, E., Berkman, M. B., Honaker, J., Ojeda, C., and Whitesell, A. (2019). Measuring Complex State Policies: Pitfalls and Considerations, with an Application to Race and Welfare Policy. *Policy Studies Journal*, **47**(3), 712–34.

Polsby, N. W. (1975). Legislatures. In F. I. Greenstein and N. W. Polsby, eds., *Governmental Institutions and Processes*. Reading, MA: Addison-Wesley, pp. 257–319.

Reich, G. (2019). One Model Does Not Fit All: The Varied Politics of State Immigration Policies, 2005–16. *Policy Studies Journal*, **47**(3), 544–71.

Rigby, E. 2012. State Resistance to 'Obamacare'. *The Forum*, **10**(2), 5.

Robinson, W. S. (1950). Ecological Correlations and the Behavior of Individuals. *American Sociological Review*, **15**(3), 351–7.

Roch, C. H., and Howard, R. M. (2008). State Policy Innovation in Perspective. *Political Research Quarterly*, **61**(2), 333–44.

Rogers, E. M. (2003). *Diffusion of Innovations*, 5th ed., New York: Free Press.

Rom, M. C., Peterson P. E., and Scheve, Jr., K. F. (1998). Interstate Competition and Welfare Policy. *Publius*, **28**(3), 17–37.

Rose, D. D. (1973). National and Local Forces in State Politics: The Implications of Multi-Level Policy Analysis. *American Political Science Review*, **67**(4), 1162–73.

Rose, R. (1991). What Is Lesson-Drawing? *Journal of Public Policy*, **11**(1), 3–30.

Rosenthal, A. (2008). *Engines of Democracy: Politics and Policymaking in State Legislatures*. Washington, DC: CQ Press.

Salisbury, R. H. (1984). Interest Representation: The Dominance of Institutions. *American Political Science Review*, **78**(1), 64–76.

Savage, R. L. (1978). Policy Innovativeness as a Trait of American States. *Journal of Politics*, **40**(1), 212–24.

Savage, R. L. (1985). Diffusion Research Traditions and the Spread of Policy Innovations in a Federal System. *Publius*, **15**(4), 1–28.

Sharkansky, I. (1968). *Spending in the American States*. Chicago: Rand-McNally.

Shipan, C. R., and Volden, C. (2006). Bottom-Up Federalism: The Diffusion of Anti-Smoking Policies from U.S. Cities to States. *American Journal of Political Science*, **50**(4), 825–43.

Shipan, C. R., and Volden, C. (2008). The Mechanisms of Policy Diffusion. *American Journal of Political Science*, **52**(4), 840–57.

Shipan, C. R., and Volden, C. (2012). Policy Diffusion: Seven Lessons for Scholars and Practitioners. *Public Administration Review*, **72**(6), 788–96.

Shipan, C. R., and Volden, C. (2014). When the Smoke Clears: Expertise, Learning and Policy Diffusion. *Journal of Public Policy*, **34**(3), 357–87.

Sigelman, L. (2006). The *American Political Science Review* Citation Classics. *American Political Science Review*, **100**(4), 667–69.

Simmons, B. A., Dobbin, F., and Garett, G. (2006). Introduction: The International Diffusion of Liberalism. *International Organization*, **60**(4), 781–810.

Simmons, B. A., and Elkins, Z. (2004). The Globalization of Liberalization: Policy Diffusion in the International Political Economy. *American Political Science Review*, **98**(1), 171–90.

Simon, H. A. (1969). *Administrative Behavior*, 2nd ed., New York: Free Press.

Skocpol, T., Abend-Wein, M., Howard, C., and Lehman, S. G. (1993). Women's Associations and the Enactment of Mother's Pensions in the United States. *American Political Science Review*, **87**(3), 686–701.

Smith, K. B. (2019). Learning without Widespread Policy Adoption: Early Childhood Education in the American States. *Publius*, **50**(1), 1–27.

Soss, J., Schram, S. R., Vartanian, T. P., and O'Brien, E. (2001). Setting the Terms of Relief: Explaining State Policy Choices in the Devolution Revolution. *American Journal of Political Science*, **45**(2), 378–95.

Soule, S. A., and Earl, J. (2001). The Enactment of State-Level Hate Crime Law in the United States: Intrastate and Interstate Factors. *Sociological Perspectives*, **44**(3), 281–305.

Squire, P. (2017). A Squire Index Update. *State Politics and Policy Quarterly*, **17**(4), 361–71.

Squire, P., and Moncrief, G. (2015). *State Legislatures Today*, 2nd ed., Lanham, MD: Rowman & Littlefield.

Stein, R. A. (2013). *Forming a More Perfect Union: A History of the Uniform Law Commission*. New York: LexisNexis.

Stepan, A. (1999). Federalism and Democracy: Beyond the US Model. *Journal of Democracy*, **10**(4), 19–34.

Strang, D., and Soule, S. A. (1998). Diffusion in Organizations and Social Movements: From Hybrid Corn to Poison Pills. *Annual Review of Sociology*, **24**, 265–90.

Strang, D., and Tuma, N. B. (1993). Spatial and Temporal Heterogeneity in Diffusion. *American Journal of Sociology*, **99**(3), 614–39.

Strebel, F., and Widmer, T. (2012). Visibility and Facticity in Policy Diffusion: Going beyond the Prevailing Binarity. *Policy Science*, **45**(3), 385–98.

Stone, D. (1999). Learning Lessons and Transferring Policy across Time, Space and Disciplines. *Politics*, **19**(1), 51–9.

Tabor, C. S., and Lodge, M. (2006). Motivated Skepticism in the Evaluation of Political Beliefs. *American Journal of Political Science*, **50**(3), 755–69.

Tarde, G. (1903). *The Laws of Invention*, Elsie Clews Parson, trans. New York: Holt.

Taylor, J. K., Lewis, D.C., Jacobsmeier, M. L., and DiSarro, B. (2012). Context and Complexity in Policy Reinvention and Diffusion: Gay and Transgender-Inclusive Laws against Discrimination. *State Politics and Policy Quarterly*, **12**(1), 75–98.

Trein, P. (2015). *Literature Report: A Review of Policy Learning in Five Strands of Political Science Research*, INSPIRES Working Paper Series 2015, no. 26. European Community's Seventh Framework Programme.

Thom, M., and An, B. (2017). Fade to Black? Exploring Policy Enactment and Termination through the Rise and Fall of State Tax Incentives for the Motion Picture Industry. *American Politics Research*, **45**(1), 85–108.

Tiebout, C. M. (1956). A Pure Theory of Local Expenditures. *Journal of Political Economy*, **64**(5), 416–37.

Tolbert, P. S., and Zucker, L.G. (1983). Institutional Sources of Change in the Formal Structure of Organizations: The Diffusion of Civil Service Reform, 1880–1935. *Administrative Science Quarterly*, **28**(1), 22–39.

Tomz, M., Goldstein, J., and Rivers, D. (2007). Do We Really Know that the WTO Increases Trade? *American Economic Review*, **97**(5), 2005–18.

Trechsel, A. H. (2006). How to Federalize the European Union … And Why Bother. *Journal of European Public Policy*, **12**(3), 401–18.

Turner, R. C. (2003). The Political Economy of Gubernatorial Smokestack Chasing: Bad Policy and Bad Politics? *State Politics and Policy Quarterly*, **3**(3), 270–93.

Volden, C. (2002). The Politics of Competitive Federalism: A Race to the Bottom in Welfare Benefits? *American Journal of Political Science*, **46**(22), 352–63.

Volden, C. (2006). States as Policy Laboratories: Emulating Success in the Children's Health Insurance Program. *American Journal of Political Science*, **50**(2), 294–312.

Volden, C. (2016). Failures: Diffusion, Learning, and Policy Abandonment. *State Politics and Policy Quarterly*, **16**(1), 44–77.

Volden, C., Ting, M. M., and Carpenter, D. P. (2008). A Formal Model of Learning and Policy Diffusion. *American Political Science Review*, **102**(3), 319–32.

Walker, J. L. (1969). The Diffusion of Innovations among the American States. *American Political Science Review*, **63**(3), 880–99.

Walker, J. L. (1971). Innovation in State Politics. In H. Jacobs and K. N. Vines, eds., *Politics in the American States*, 2nd ed., Boston, MA: Little, Brown, pp. 354–87.

Walker, J. L. (1973). Comment (on Gray). *American Political Science Review*, **67**(4), 1186–91.

Walker, J. L. (1981). The Diffusion of Knowledge, Policy Communities and Agenda Setting: The Relationship between Knowledge and Power. In J. E. Tropman, M. J. Dluhy, and R. M. Lind, eds., *New Strategic Perspectives on Social Policy*. New York: Pergamon Press, pp. 75–96.

Walker, J. L. (1991). *Mobilizing Interest Groups in America*. Ann Arbor, MI: University of Michigan Press.

Wallis, J. L., and Oates, W. (1998). The Impact of the New Deal on American Federalism. In M. D. Bordo, C. Goldin, and E. N. White, eds., *The Defining Moment: The Great Depression and the American Economy in the Twentieth Century*. Chicago: University of Chicago Press, pp. 155–80.

Weissert, C. S. (1991). Policy Entrepreneurs, Policy Opportunists, and Legislative Effectiveness. *American Politics Quarterly*, **19**(2), 262–74.

Welch, S., and Thompson, K. (1980). The Impact of Federal Incentives on State Policy Innovation. *American Journal of Political Science*, **24**(4), 715–29.

Weyland, K. (2005). Theories of Policy Diffusion: Lessons from Latin American Pension Reform. *World Politics*, **57**(2), 262–95.

Weyland, K. (2009). *Bounded Rationality and Policy Diffusion: Social Sector Reform in Latin America*. Princeton, NJ: Princeton University Press.

Wildavsky, A. (1964). *The Politics of the Budgetary Process*. Boston: Little, Brown.

Wolman, H. (1992). Understanding Cross-National Policy Transfers: The Case of Britain and the US. *Governance*, **5**(1), 27–45.

Woods, N. D. (2006.) Interstate Competition and Environmental Regulation: A Test of the Race-to-the-Bottom Thesis. *Social Science Quarterly*, **87**(1), 174–89.

Woods, N.D. (n.d.). An Environmental Race to the Bottom? 'No More Stringent Laws' in the American States. University of South Carolina, Department of Government. Typescript.

Zhu, L., Guo, H., Zhao, Z., and Cheng, S. (N.d.) Taking Space Seriously: Comparing Multilevel and Spatial Modeling in Addressing Spatial Associations in Public Administration Research. University of Houston, Department of Political Science. Typescript.

Zimmerman, J. F. (1976). State-Local Relations: The State Mandate Irritant. *National Civic Review*, **65**(11), 548–52.

Acknowledgments

I would like to thank the following scholars for their help and support in developing this essay: Frank Baumgartner, Virginia Gray, Eric Hansen, Joshua Jansa, Andrew Karch, Rebecca Kreitzer, Daniel Mallinson, Sean Nicholson-Crotty, Isaac Pollert, Srinivas Parinandi, Chuck Shipan, Craig Volden, and Neal Woods.

As always, I dedicate this essay to Laura.

Cambridge Elements ≡

American Politics

Frances E. Lee
Princeton University
Frances E. Lee is Professor of Politics at the Woodrow Wilson School of Princeton University. She is author of *Insecure Majorities: Congress and the Perpetual Campaign* (2016), *Beyond Ideology: Politics, Principles and Partisanship in the U.S. Senate* (2009), and coauthor of *Sizing Up the Senate: The Unequal Consequences of Equal Representation* (1999).

Advisory Board

About the Series

The Cambridge Elements Series in *American Politics* publishes authoritative contributions on American politics. Emphasizing works that address big, topical questions within the American political landscape, the series is open to all branches of the subfield and actively welcomes works that bridge subject domains. It publishes both original new research on topics likely to be of interest to a broad audience and state-of-the-art synthesis and reconsideration pieces that address salient questions and incorporate new data and cases to inform arguments.

American Politics

Elements in the series

A full series listing is available at: www.cambridge.org/core/series/elements-in-american-politics

Printed in the United States
By Bookmasters